I0433648

Two Seas

Two Seas
Volume II

Berlin: The Living and the Dead

Peter Shaindlin

DEUXMERS

Published by Deuxmers, LLC
PO Box 440, Waimanalo, Hawaii.

Photographed in Berlin between 2014 and 2016.

Printed in the United States of America.
ISBN: 978-1-944521-04-2
First edition, May 2017

Plaudite, amici, comedia finita est.

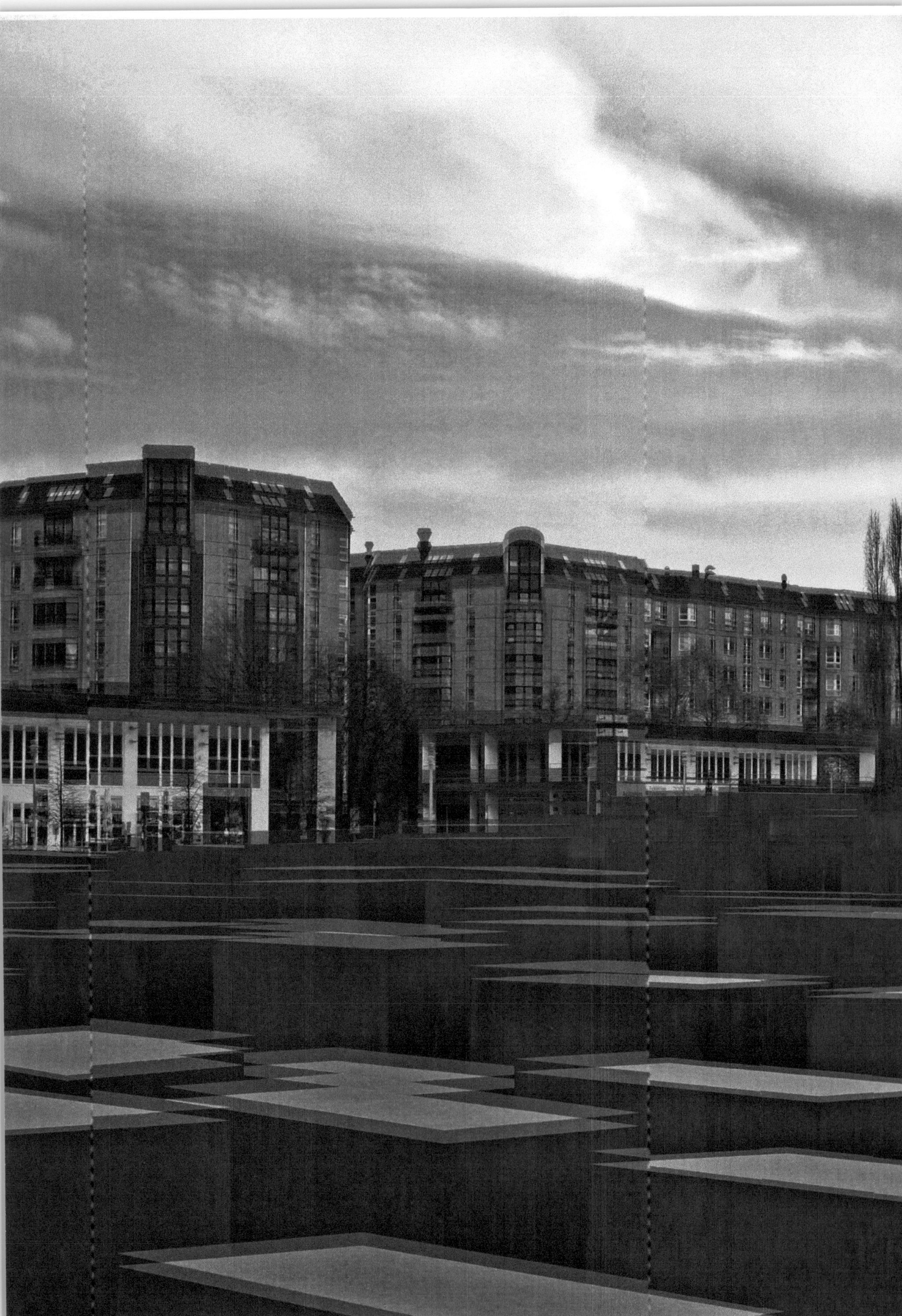

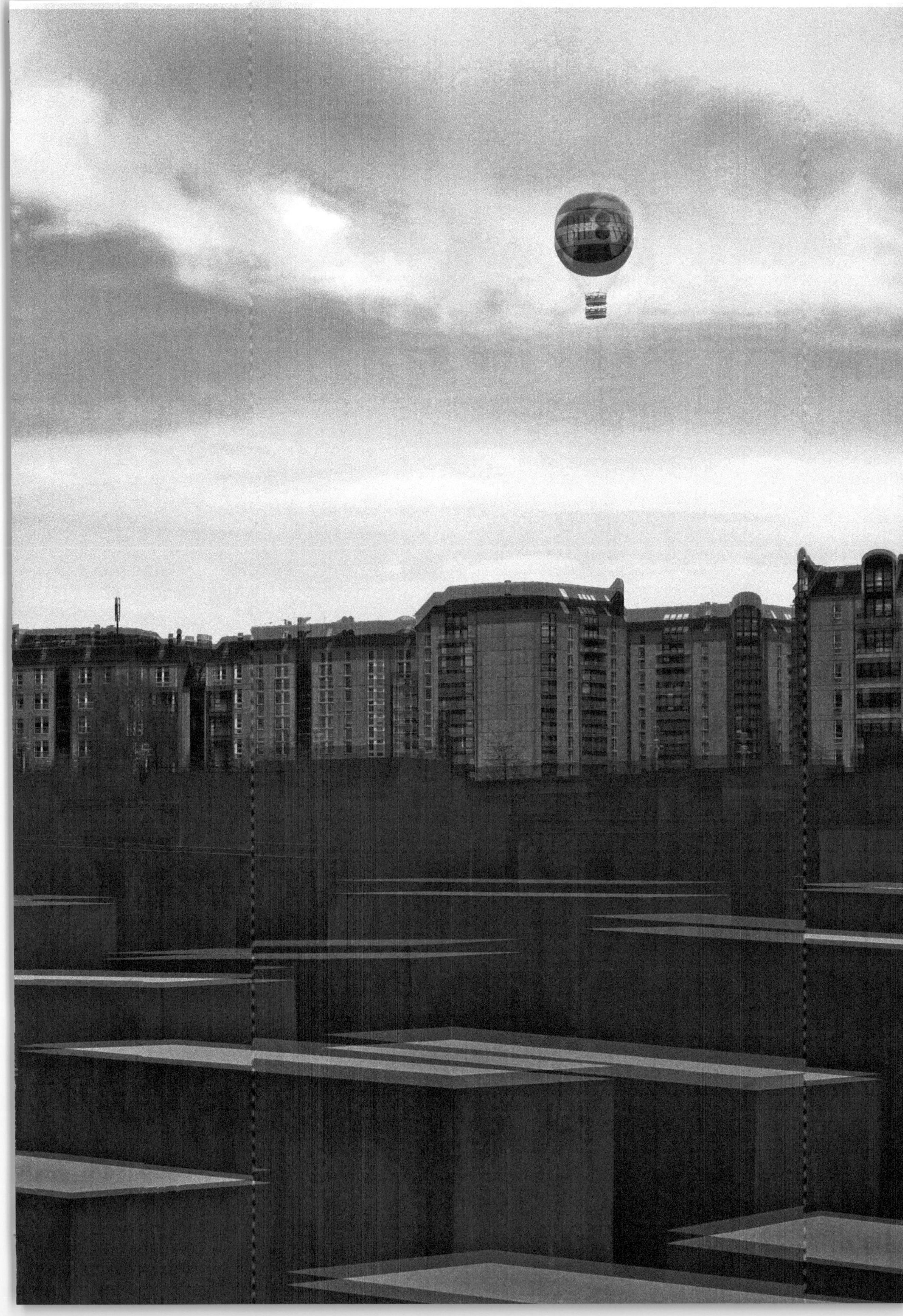

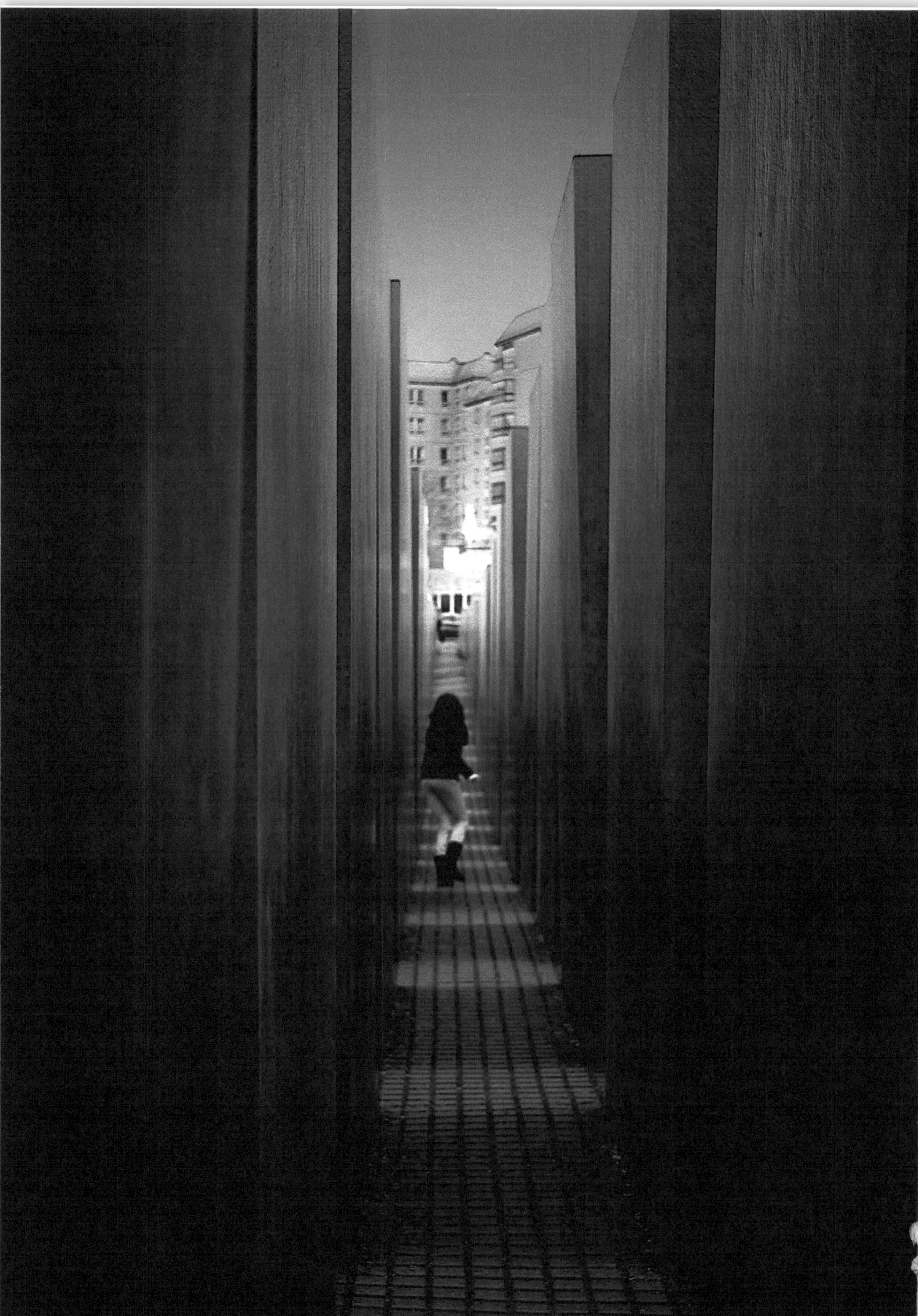

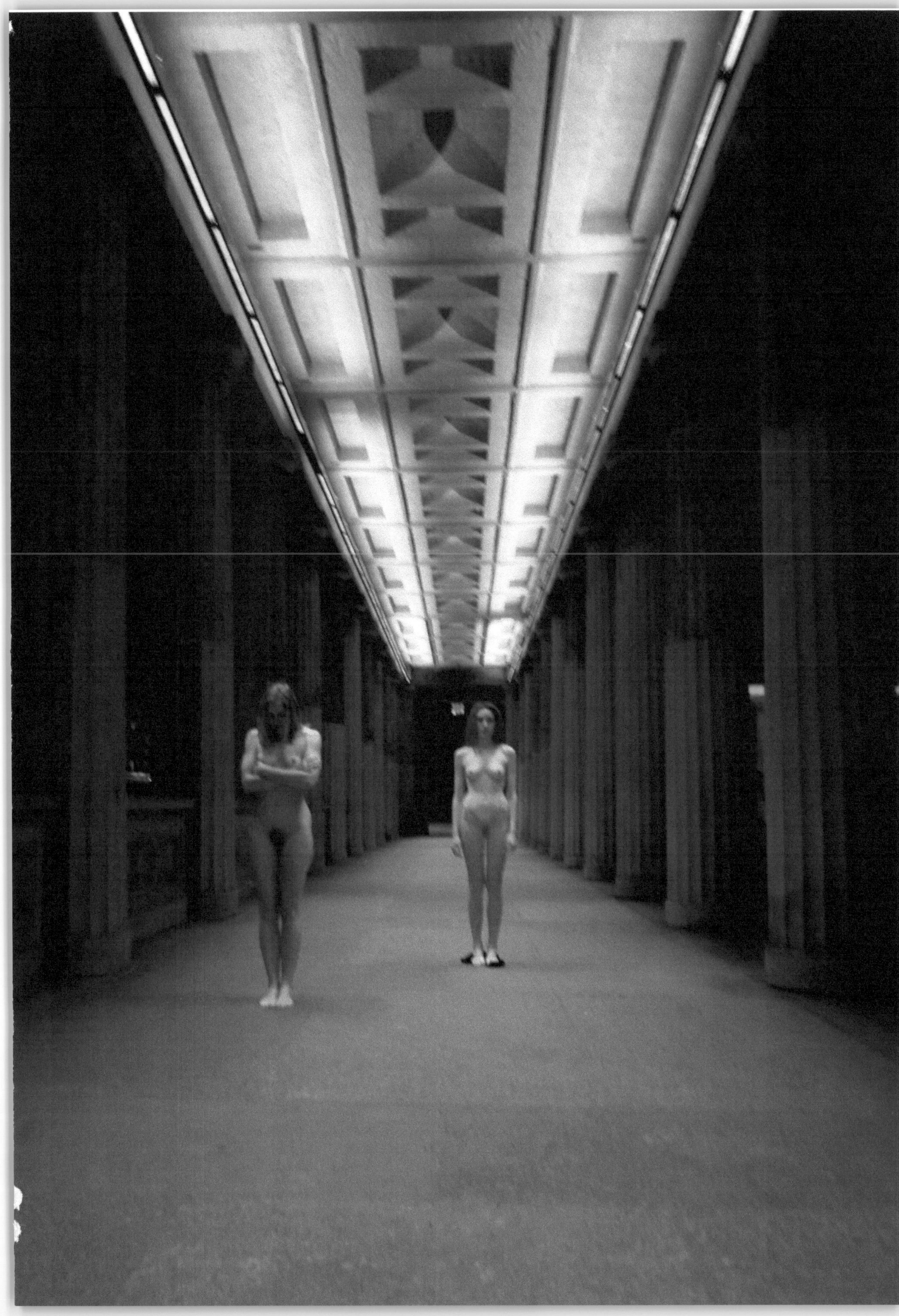

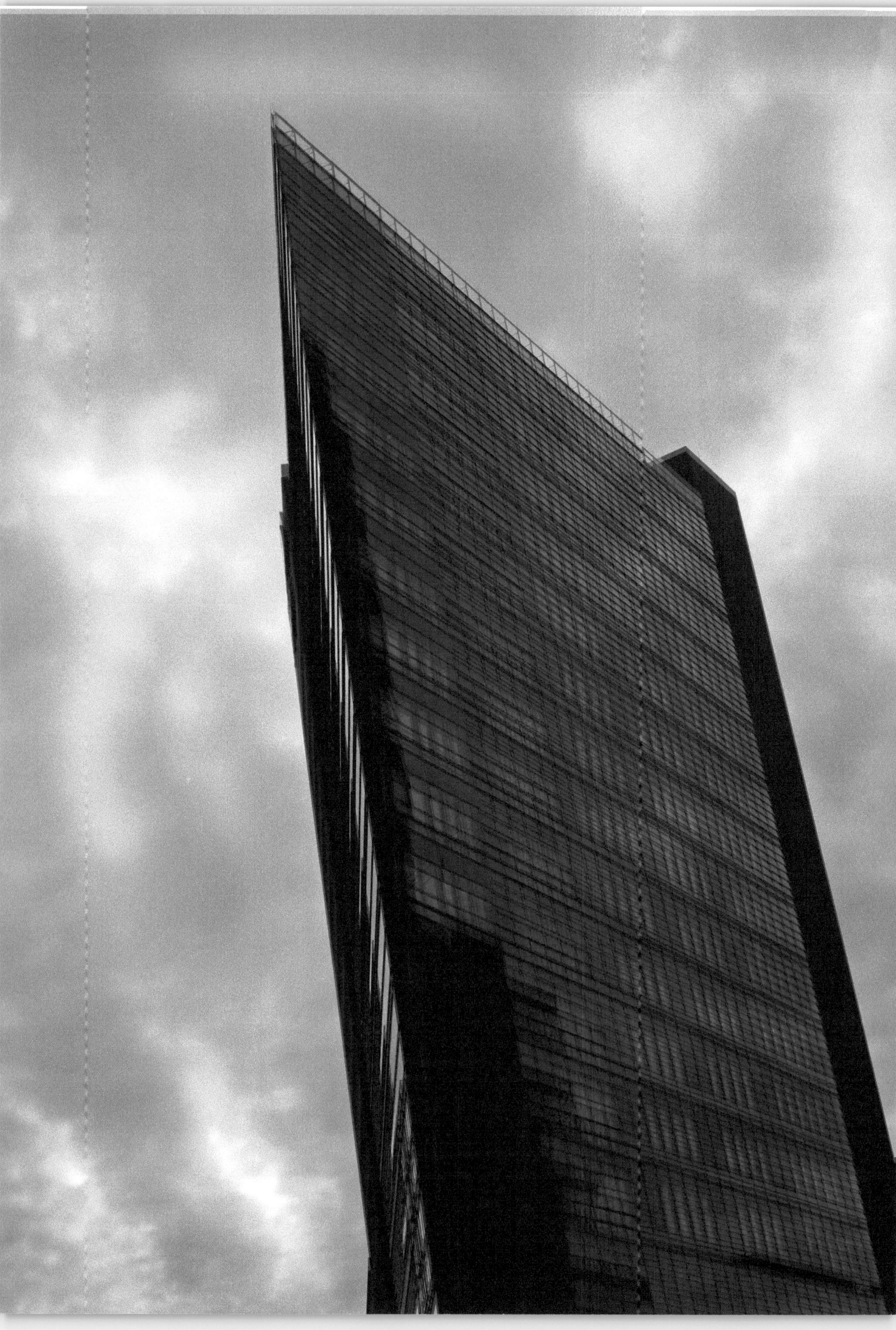

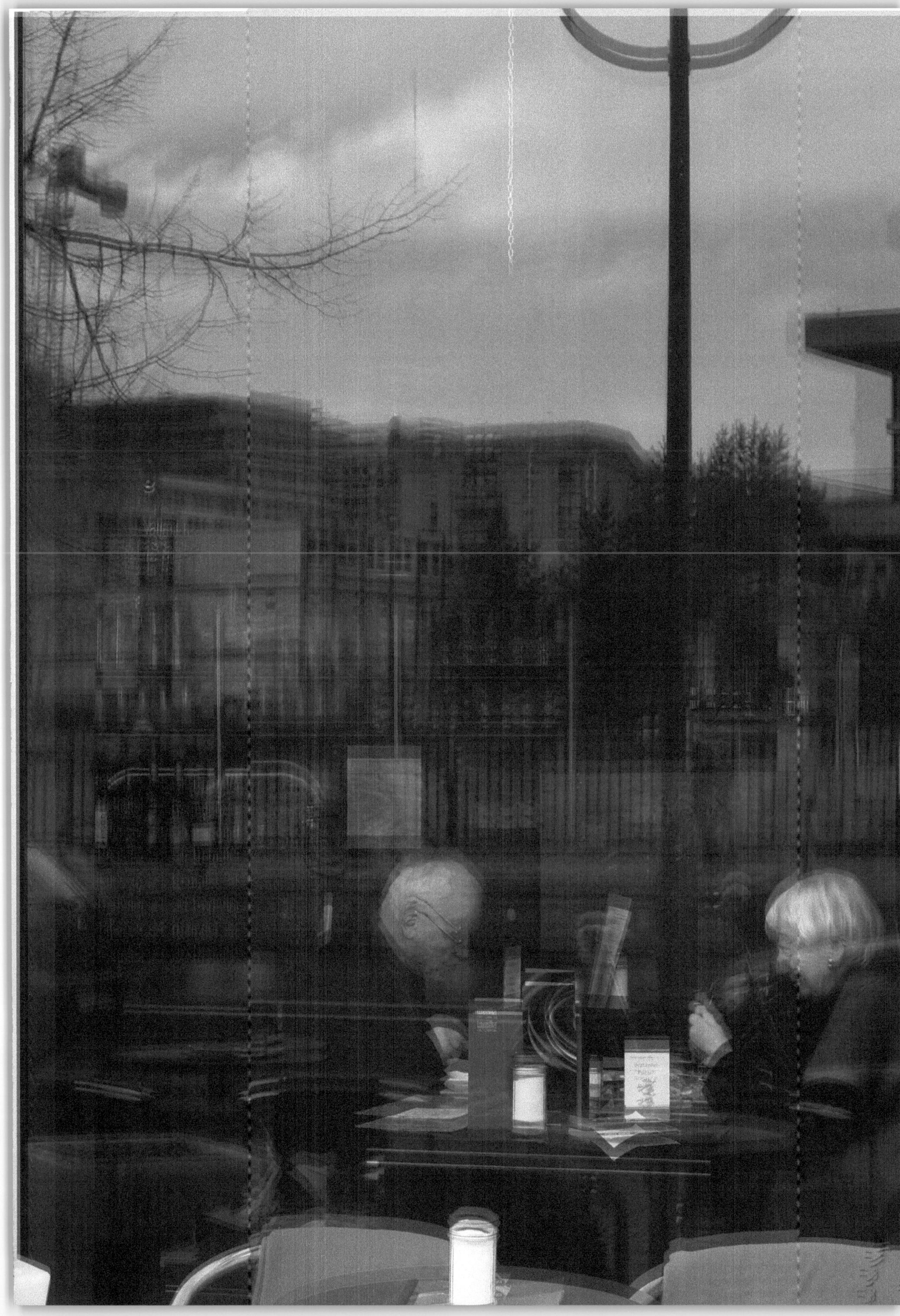

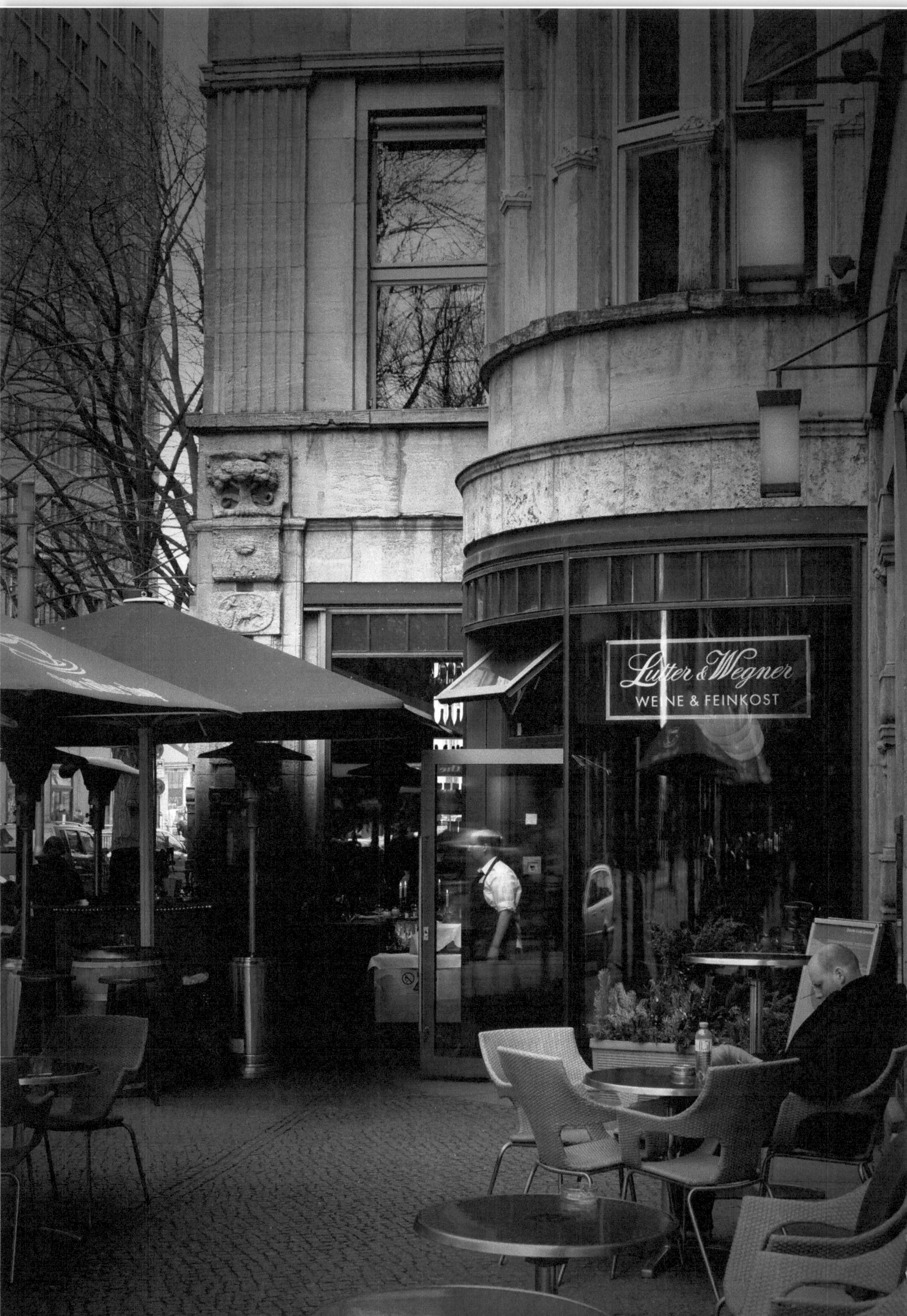
Lutter & Wegner
WEINE & FEINKOST

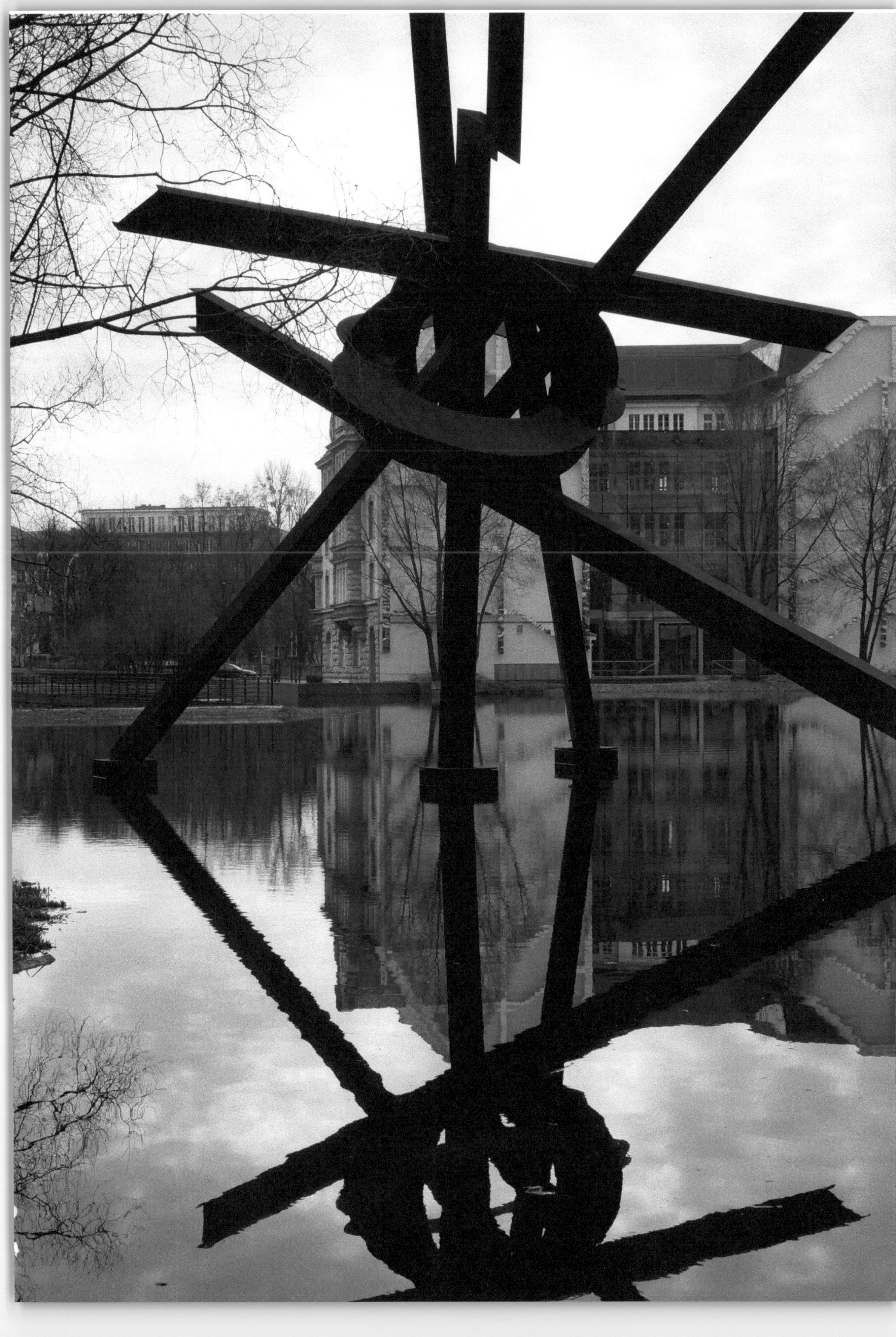

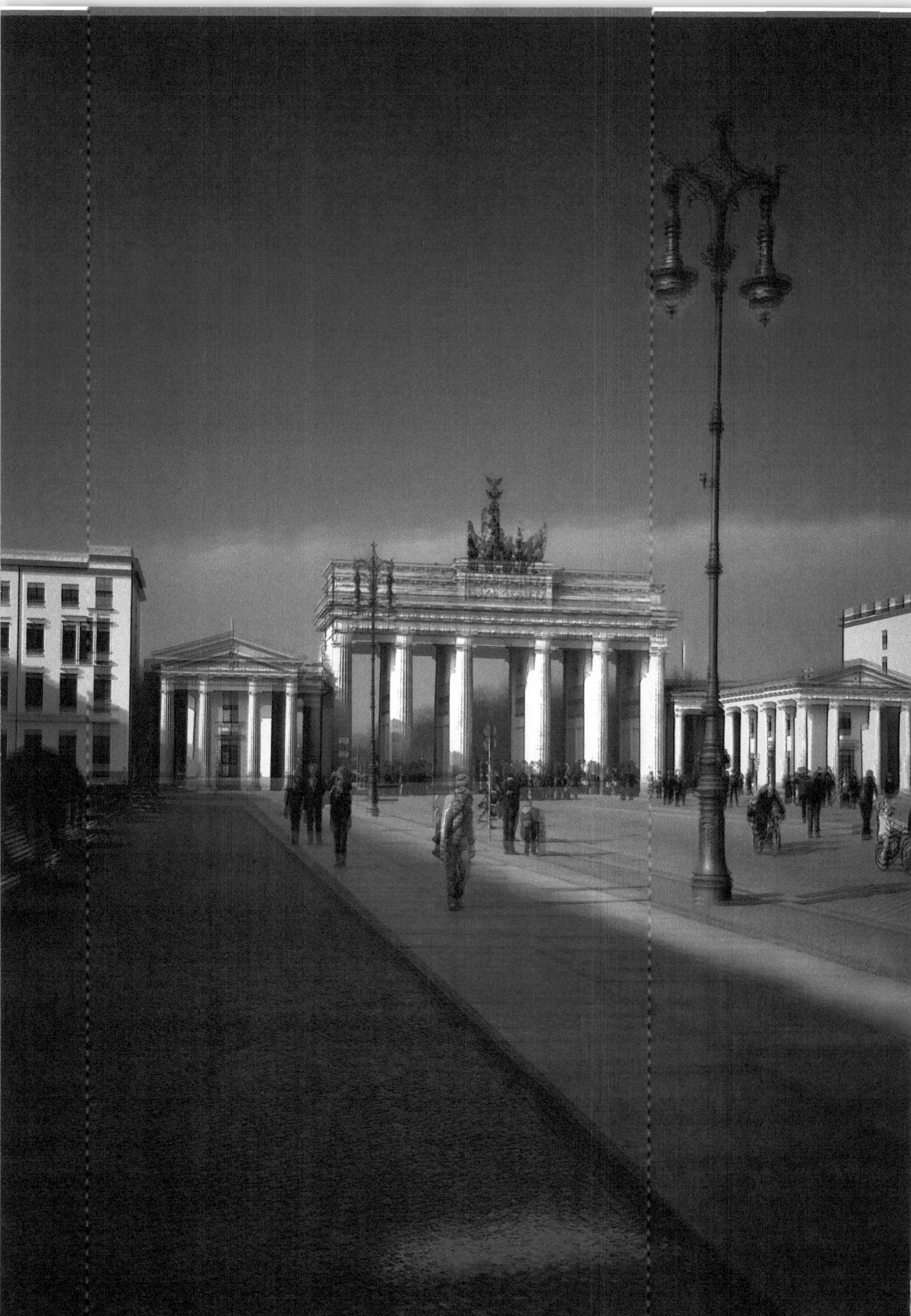

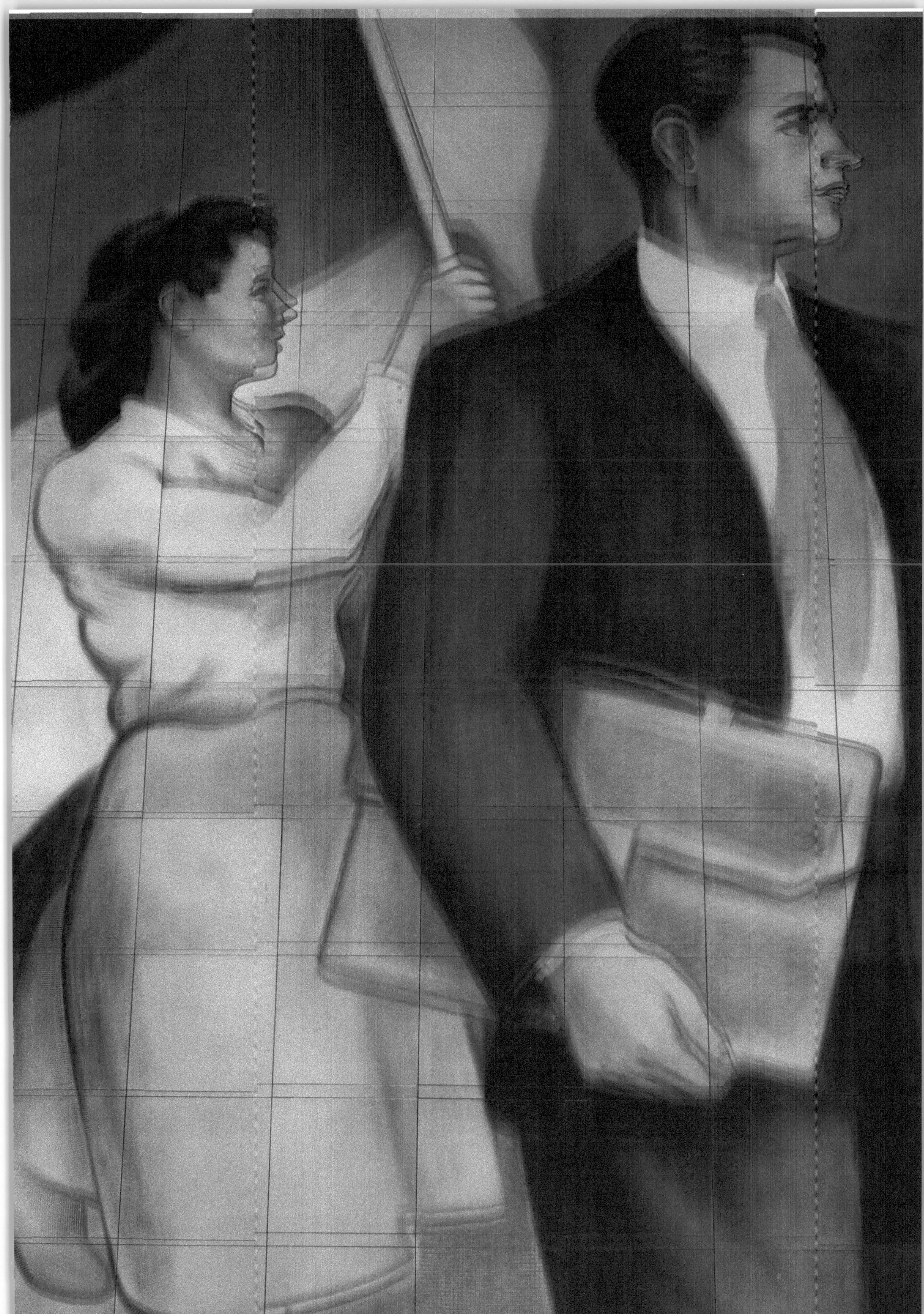

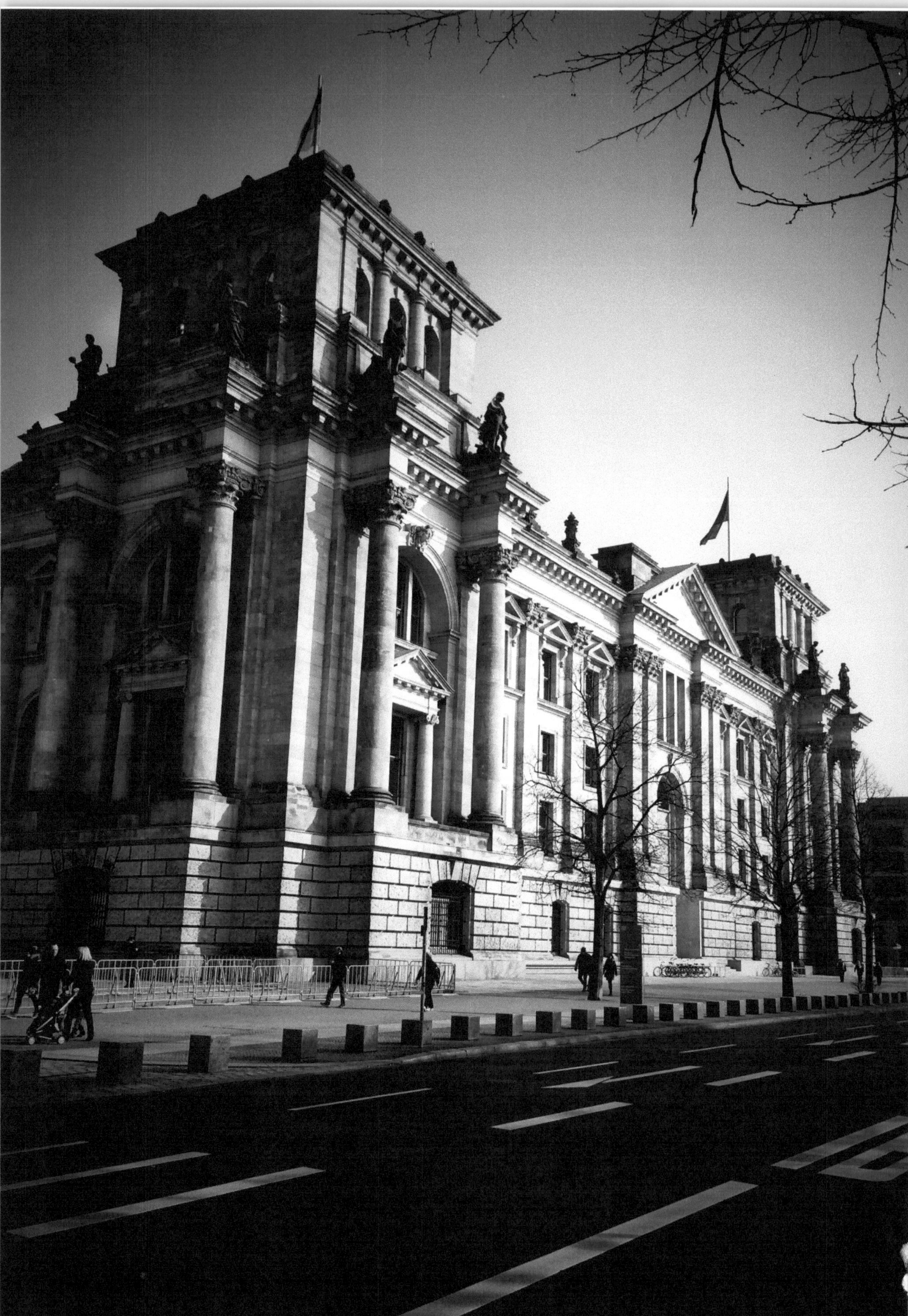

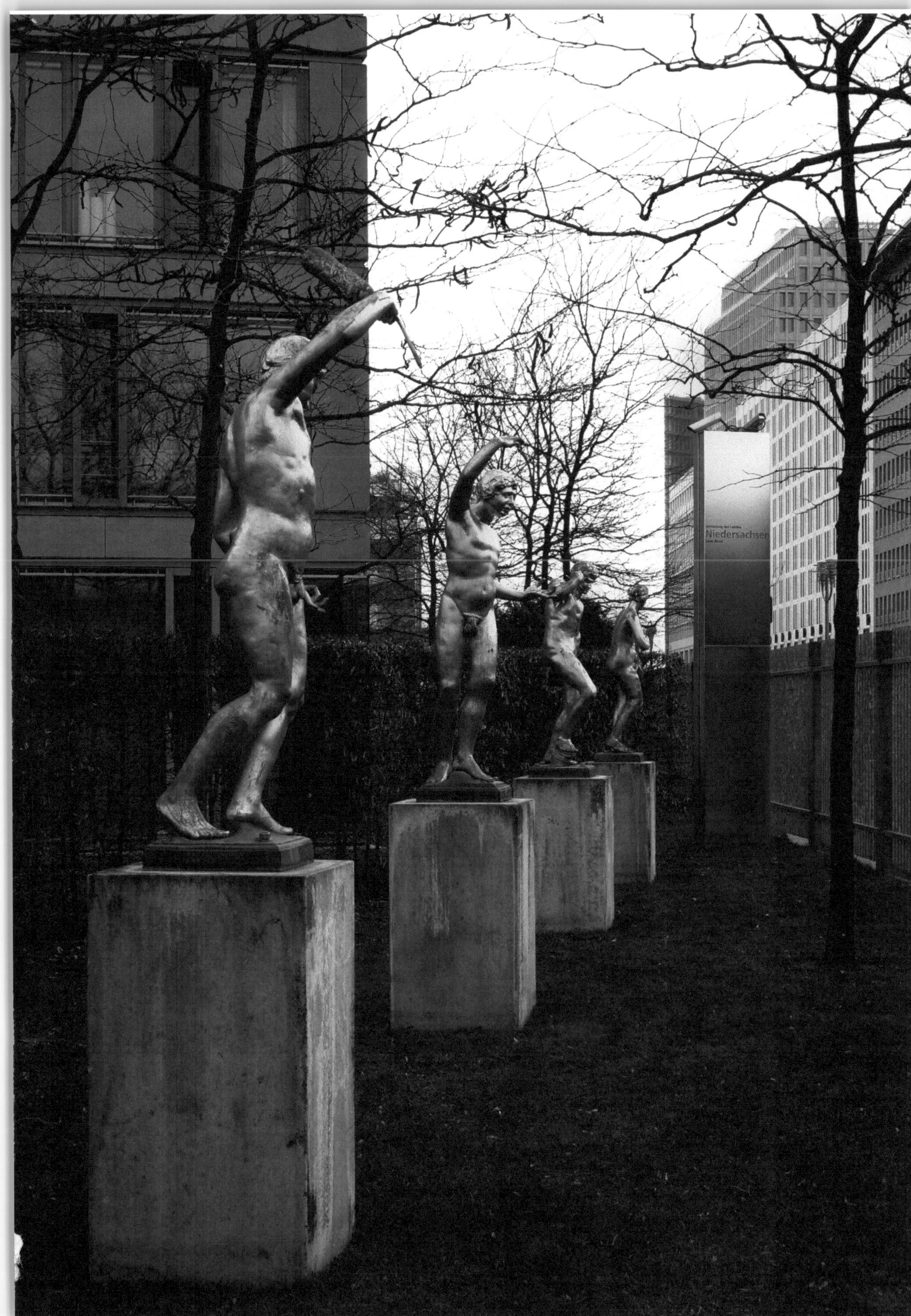
Niedersachsen

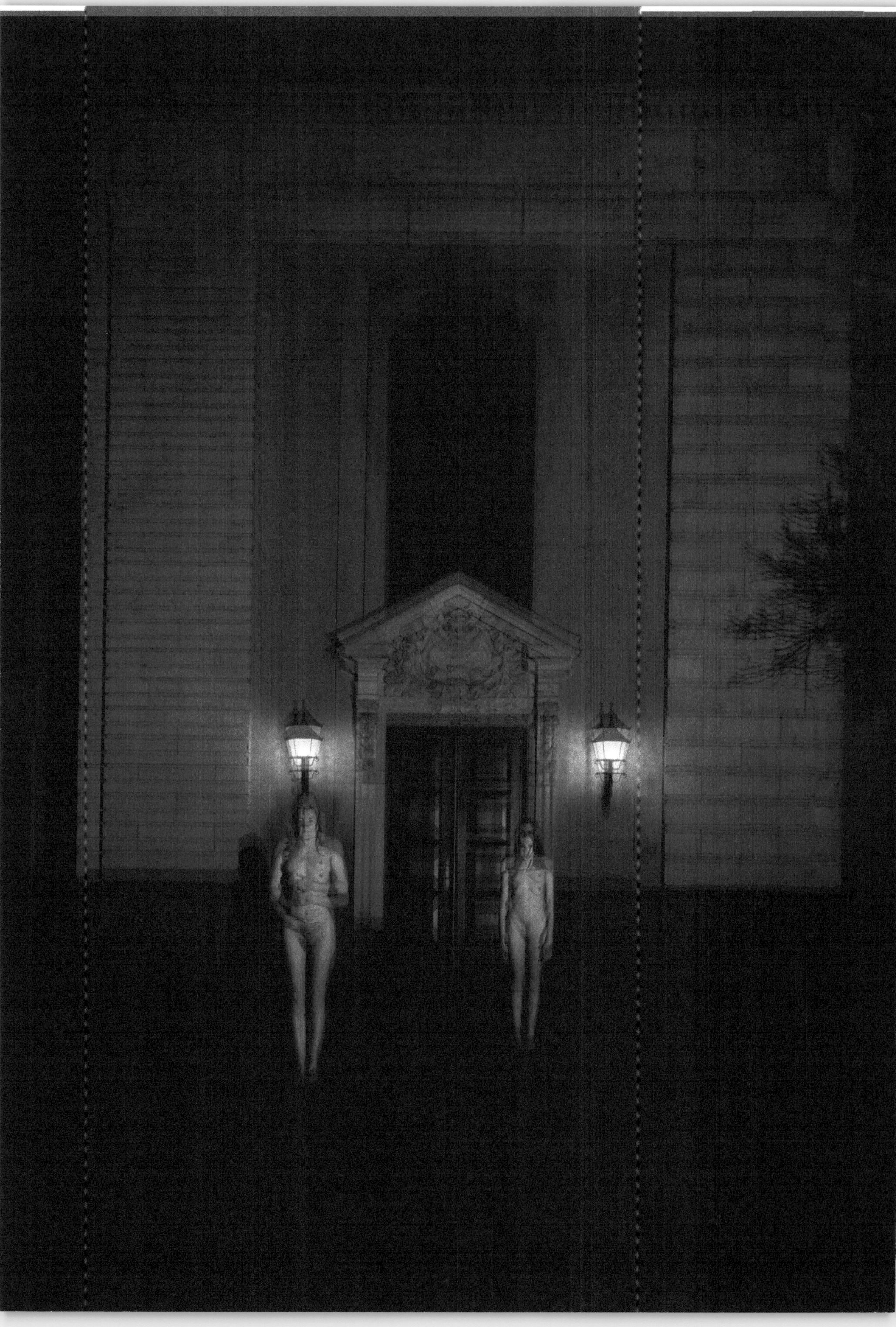

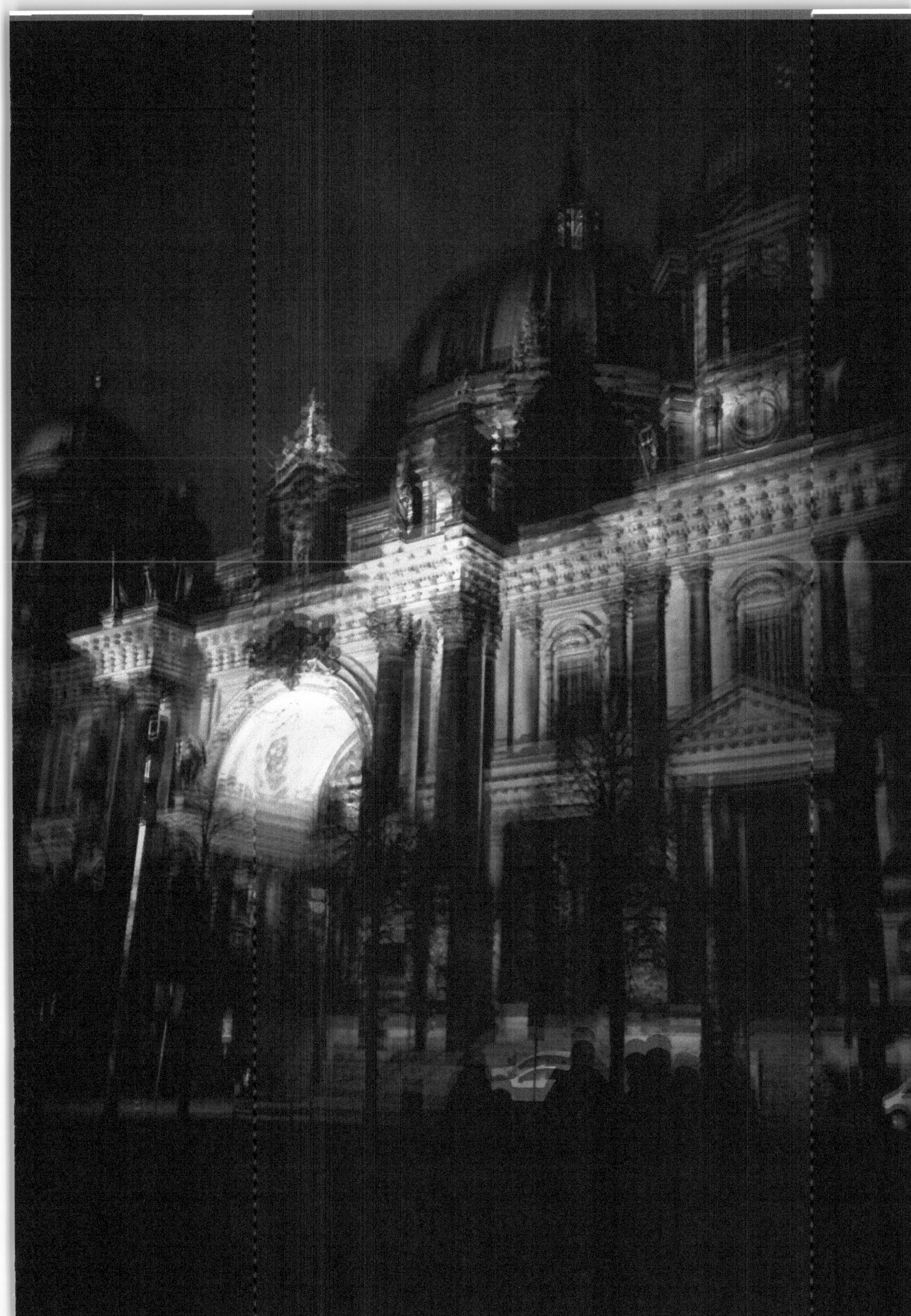

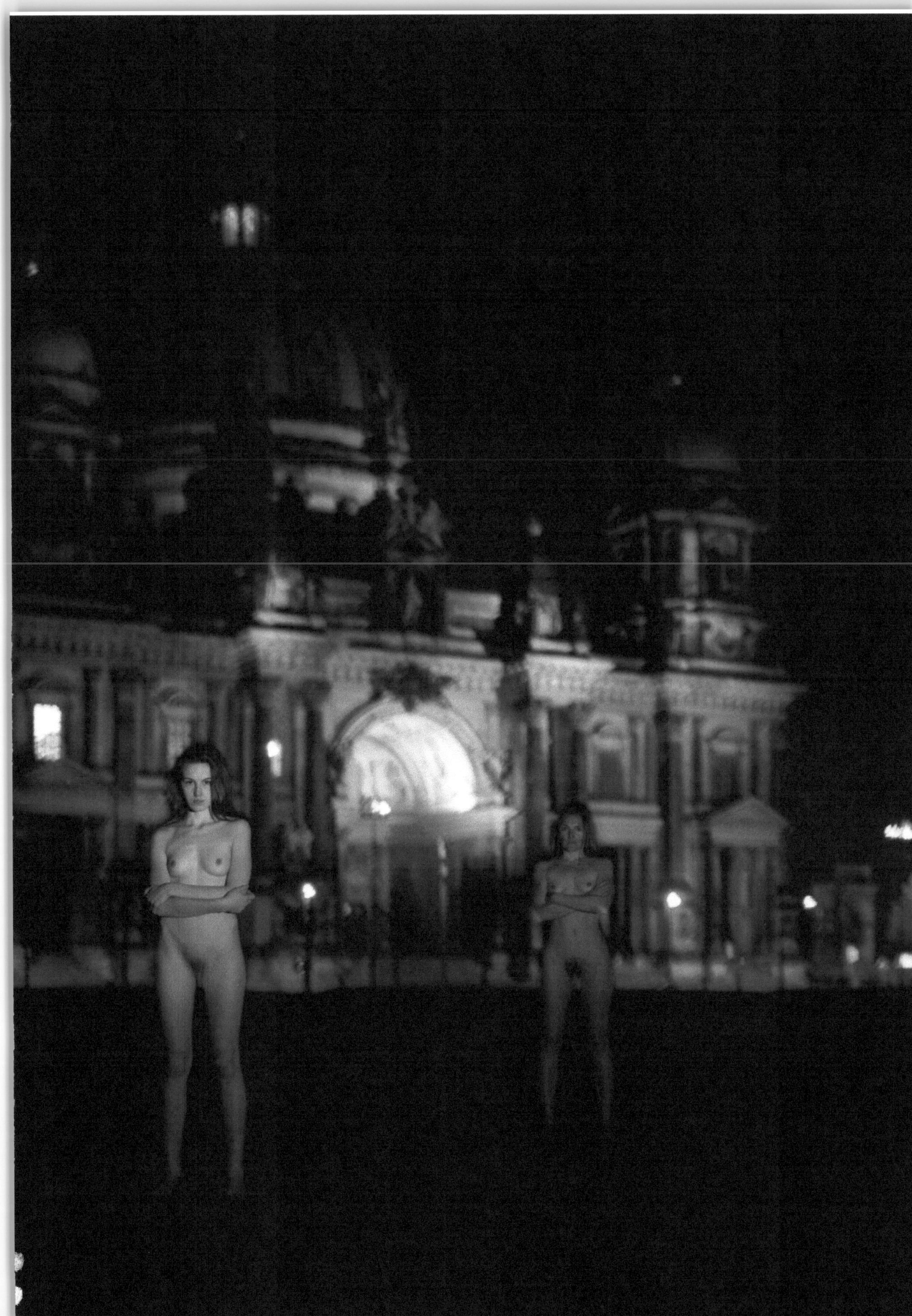

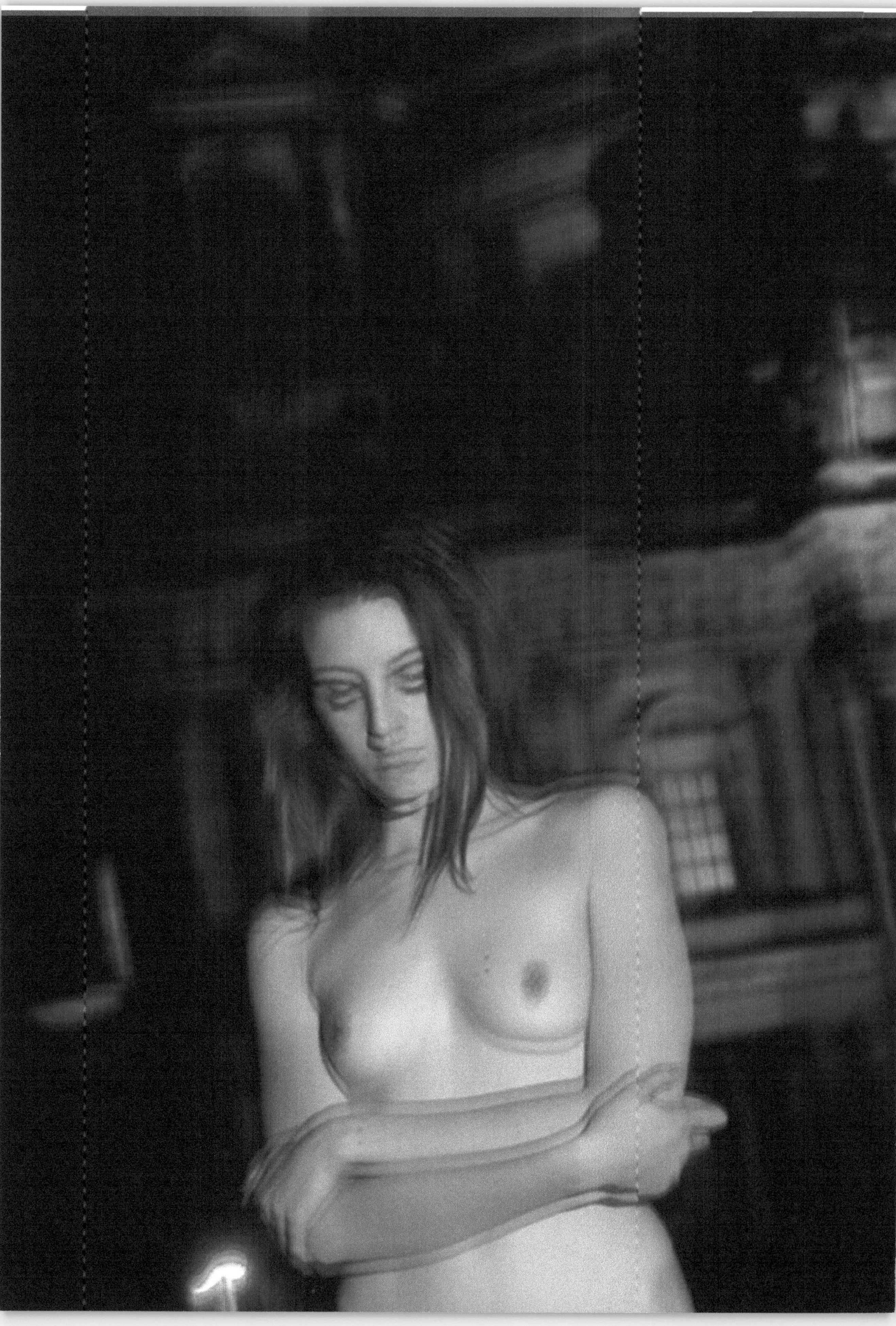

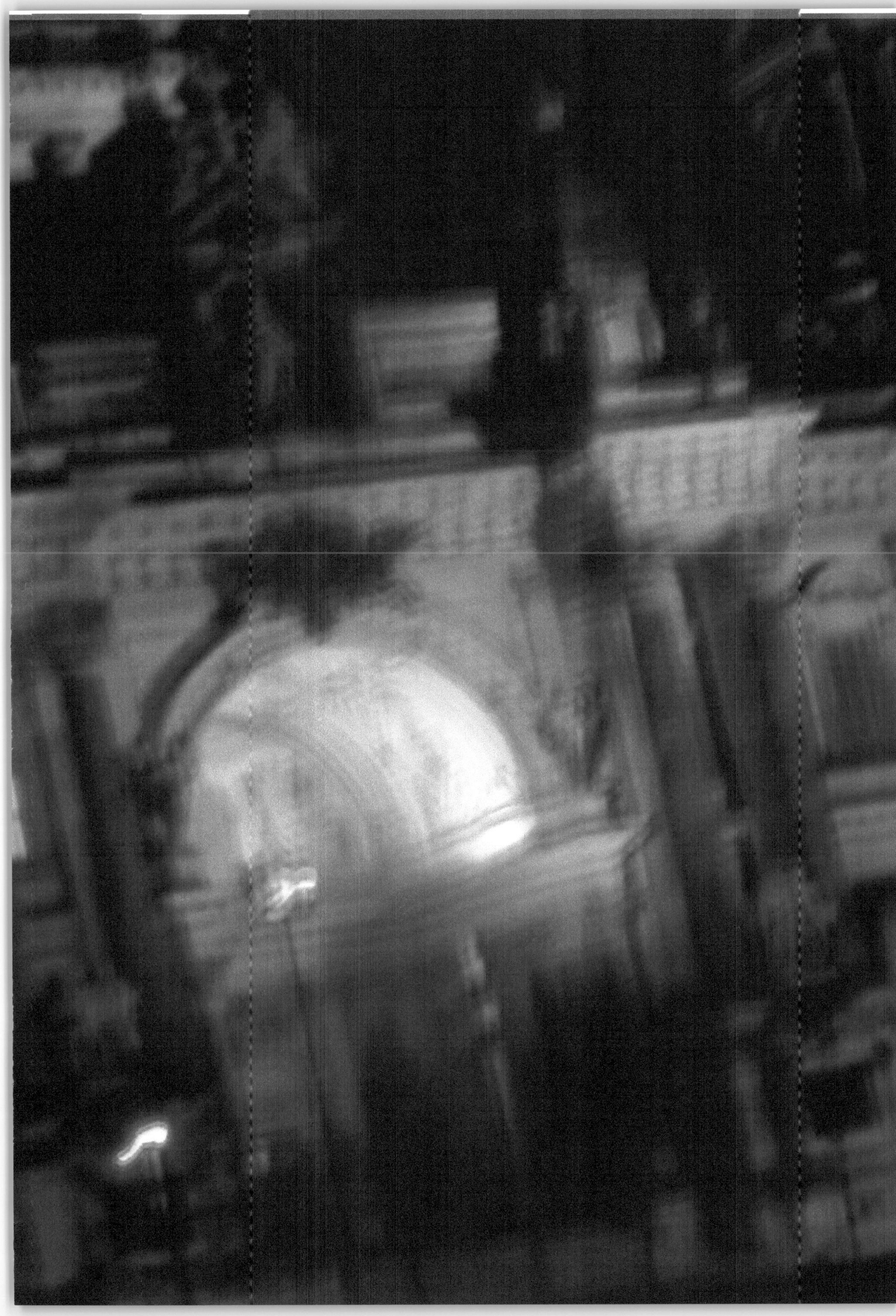

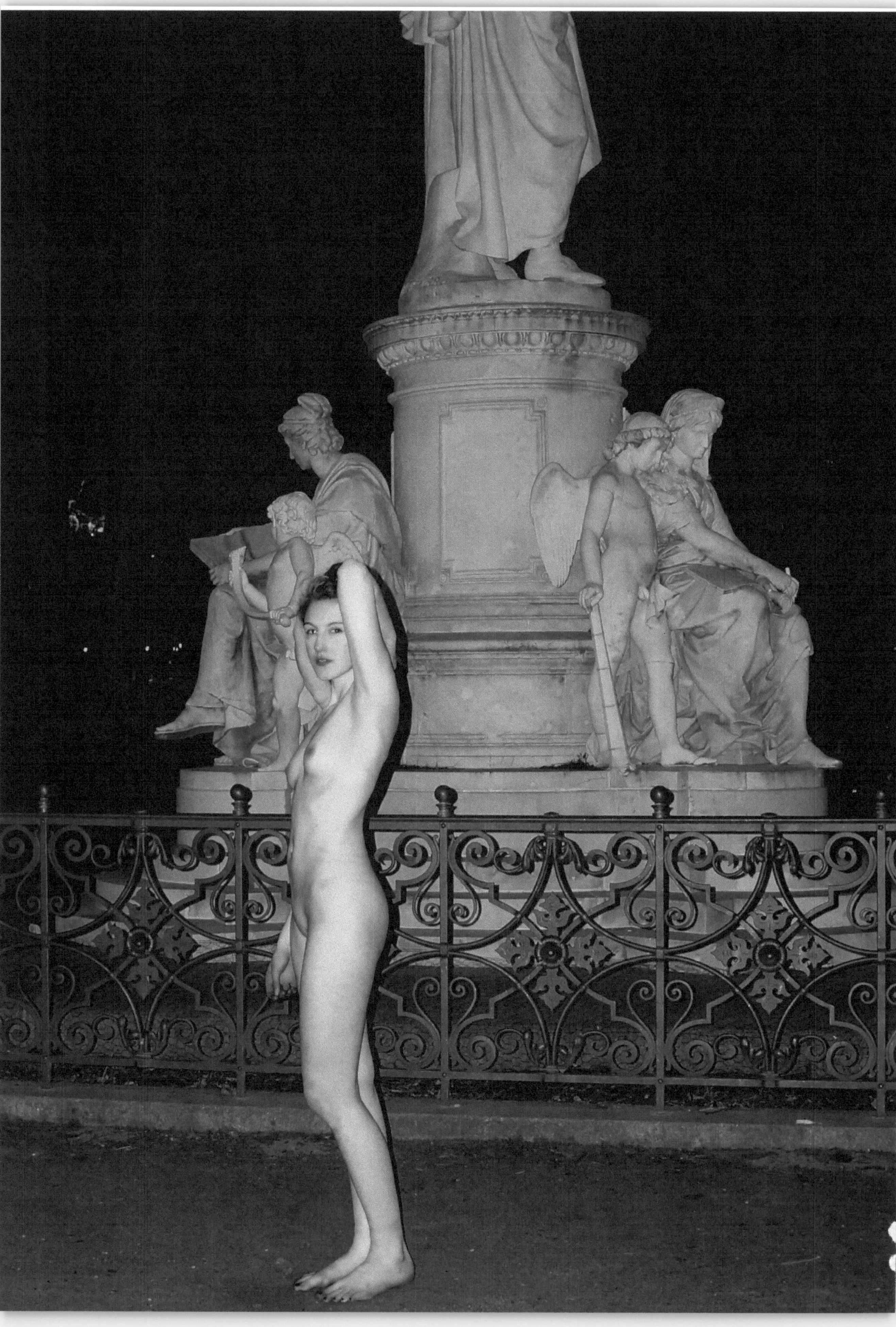

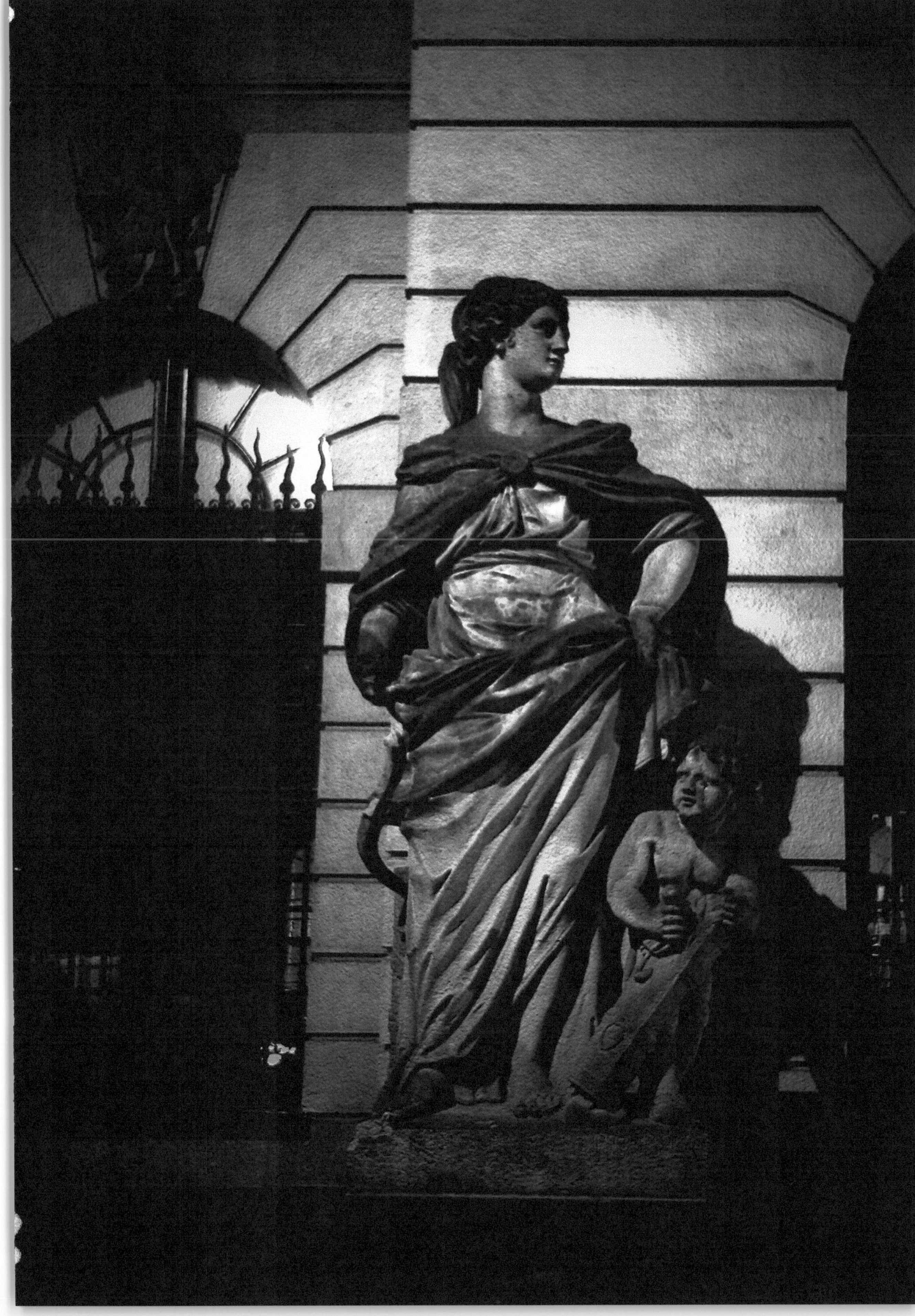

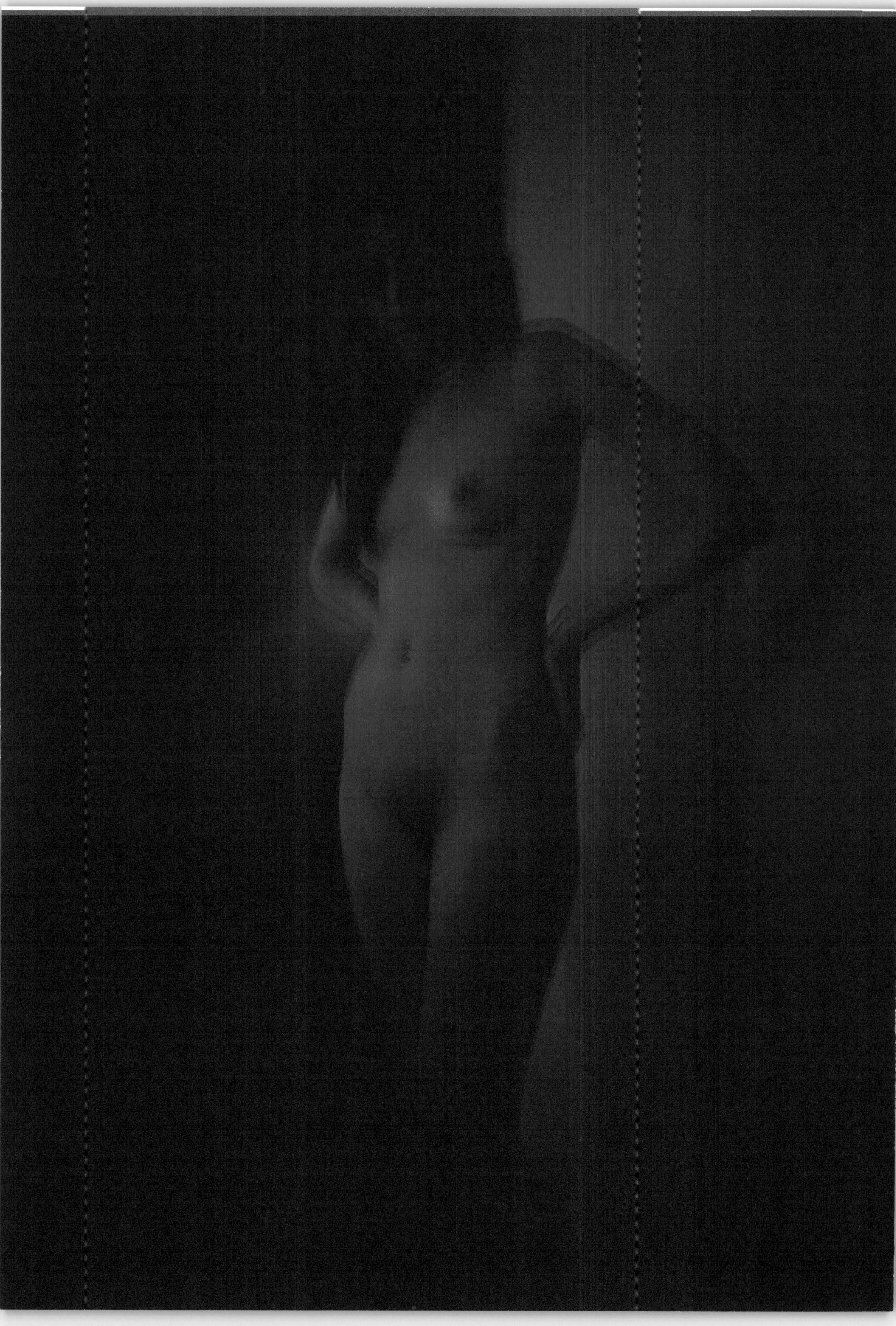

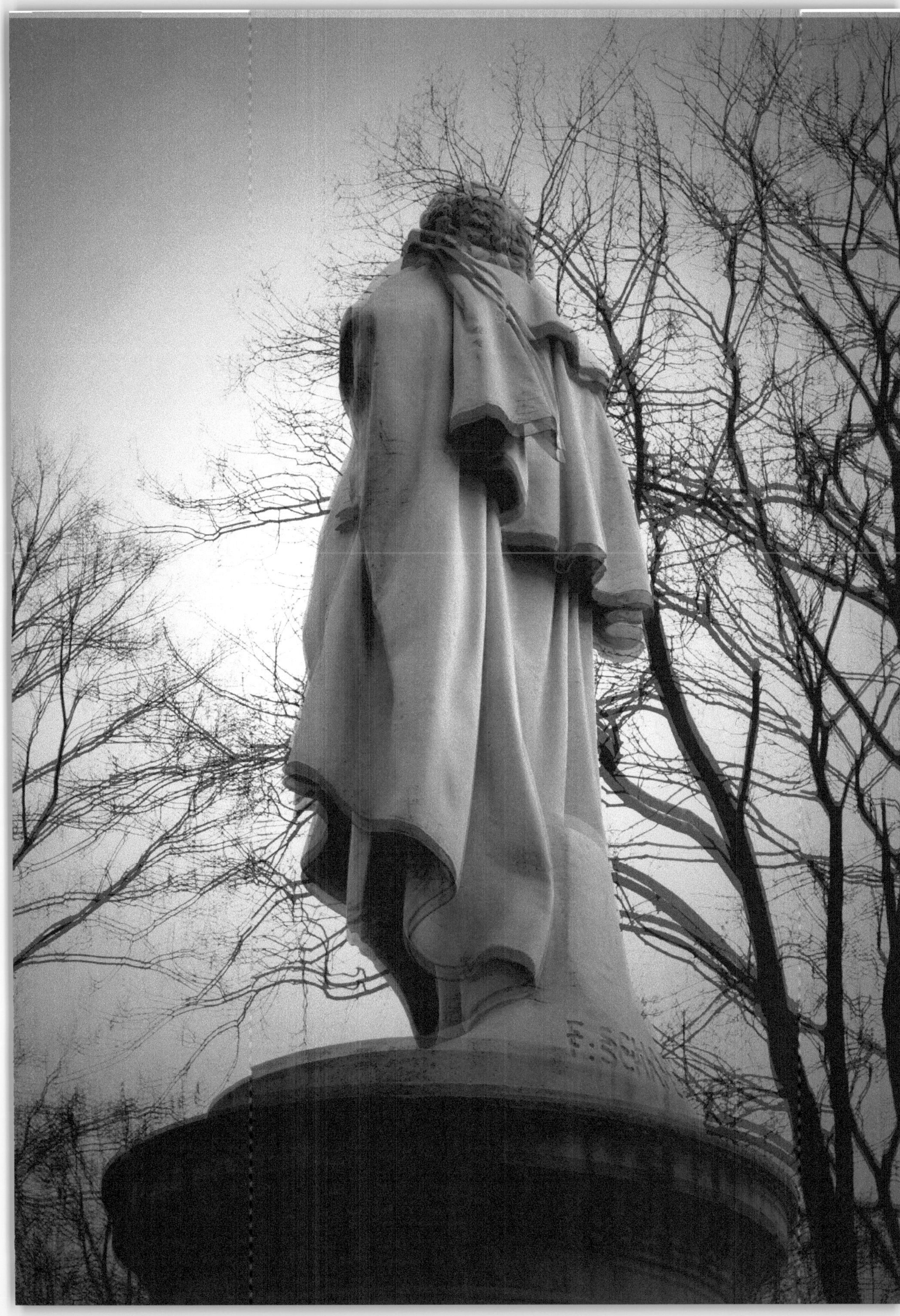

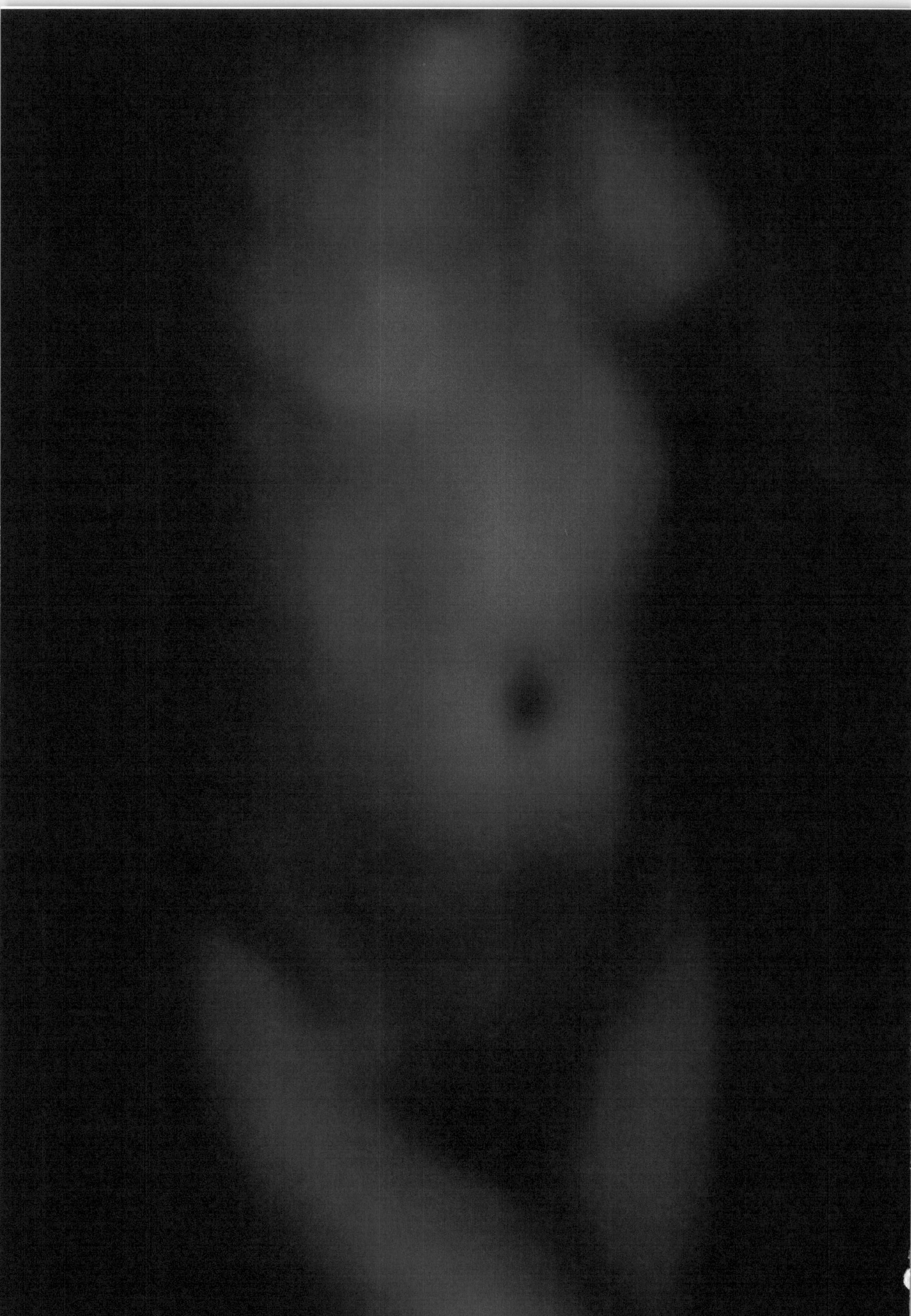

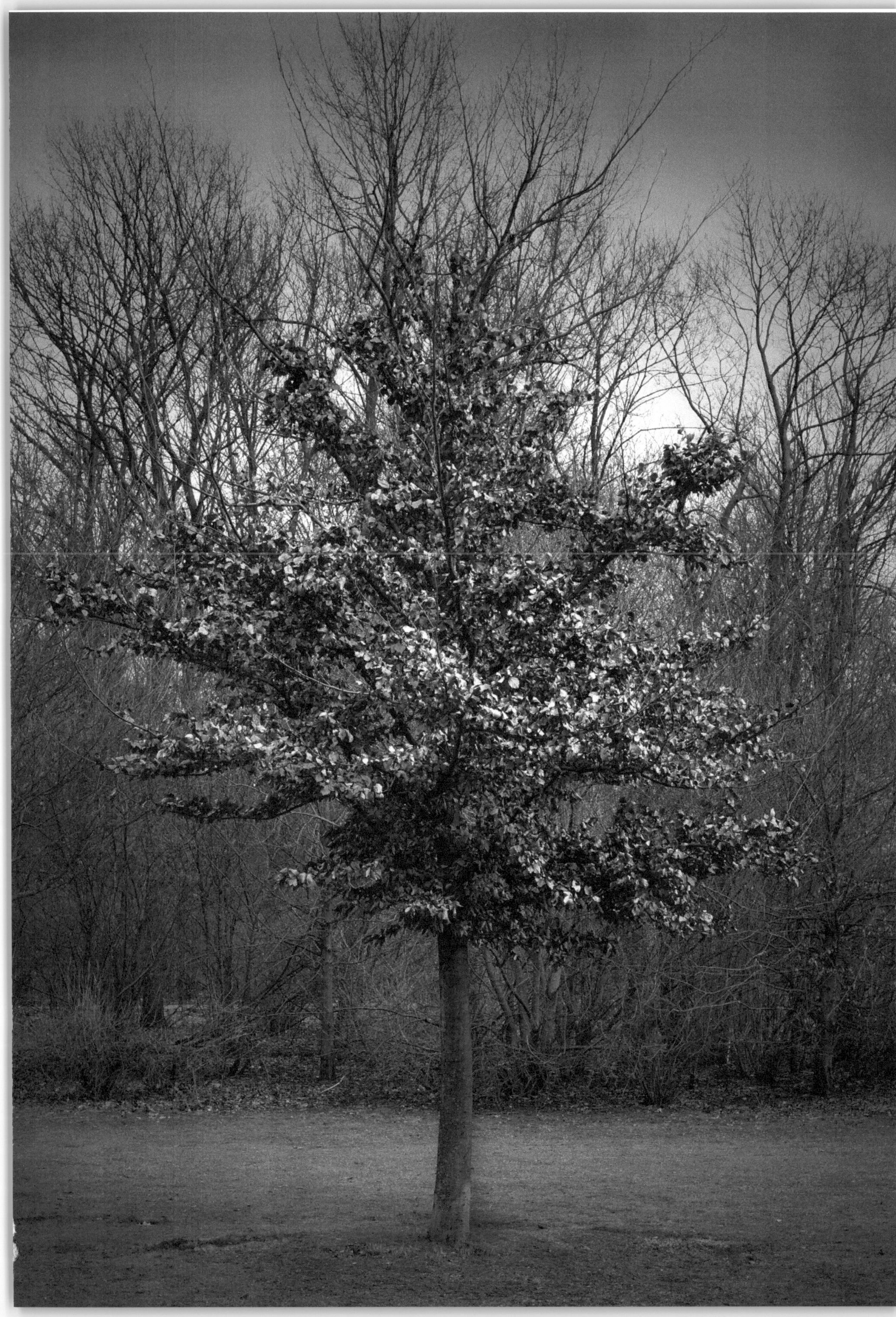

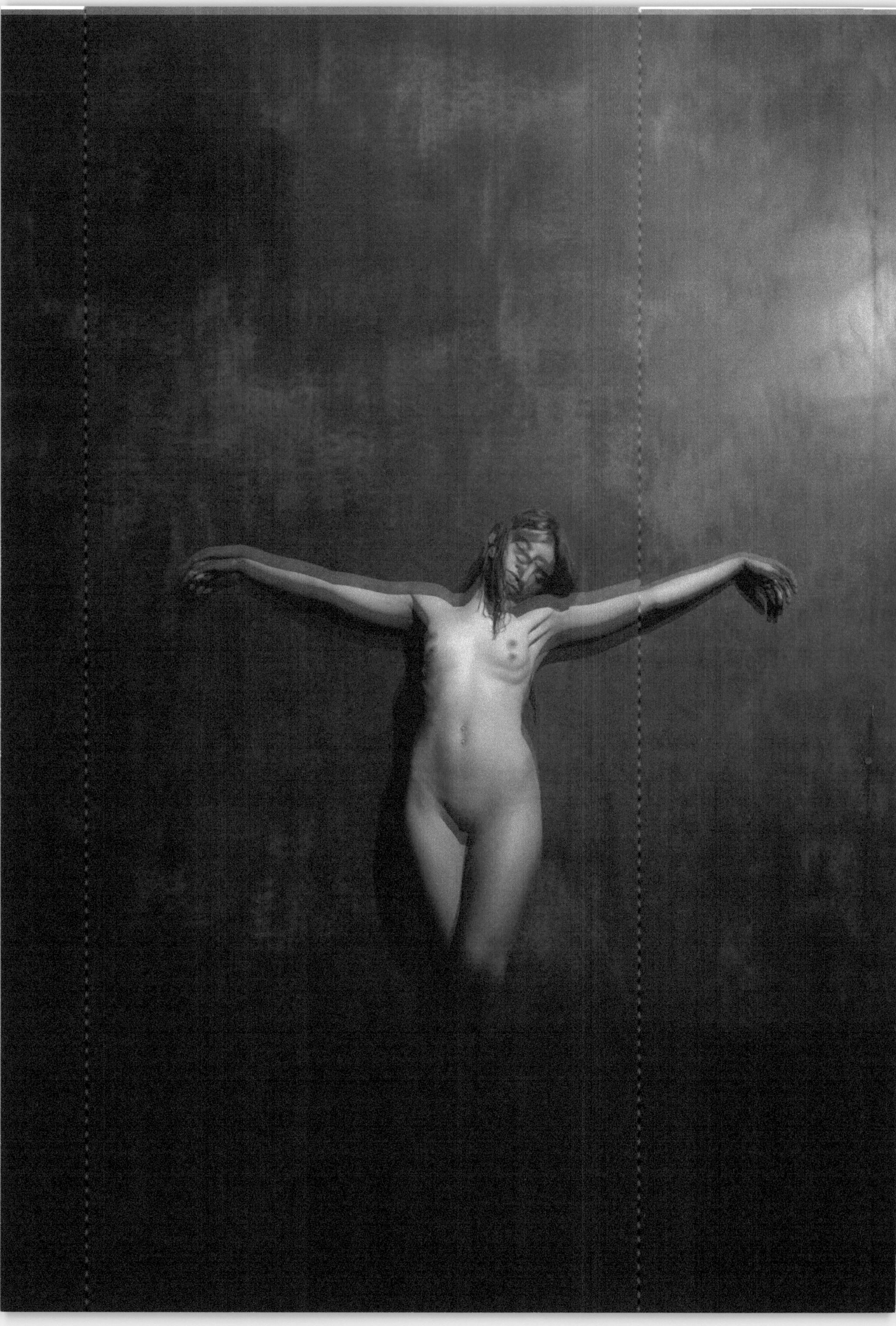

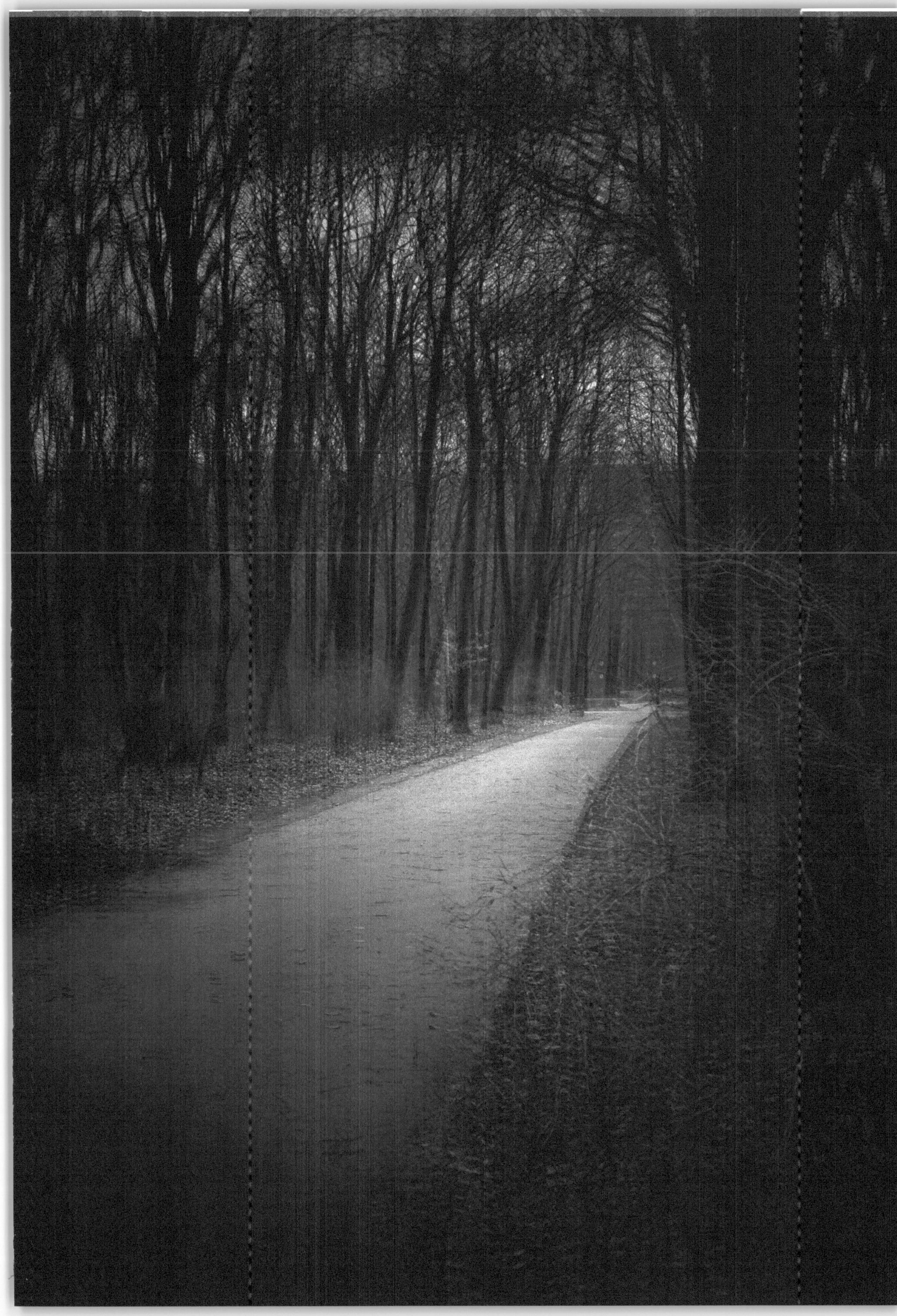

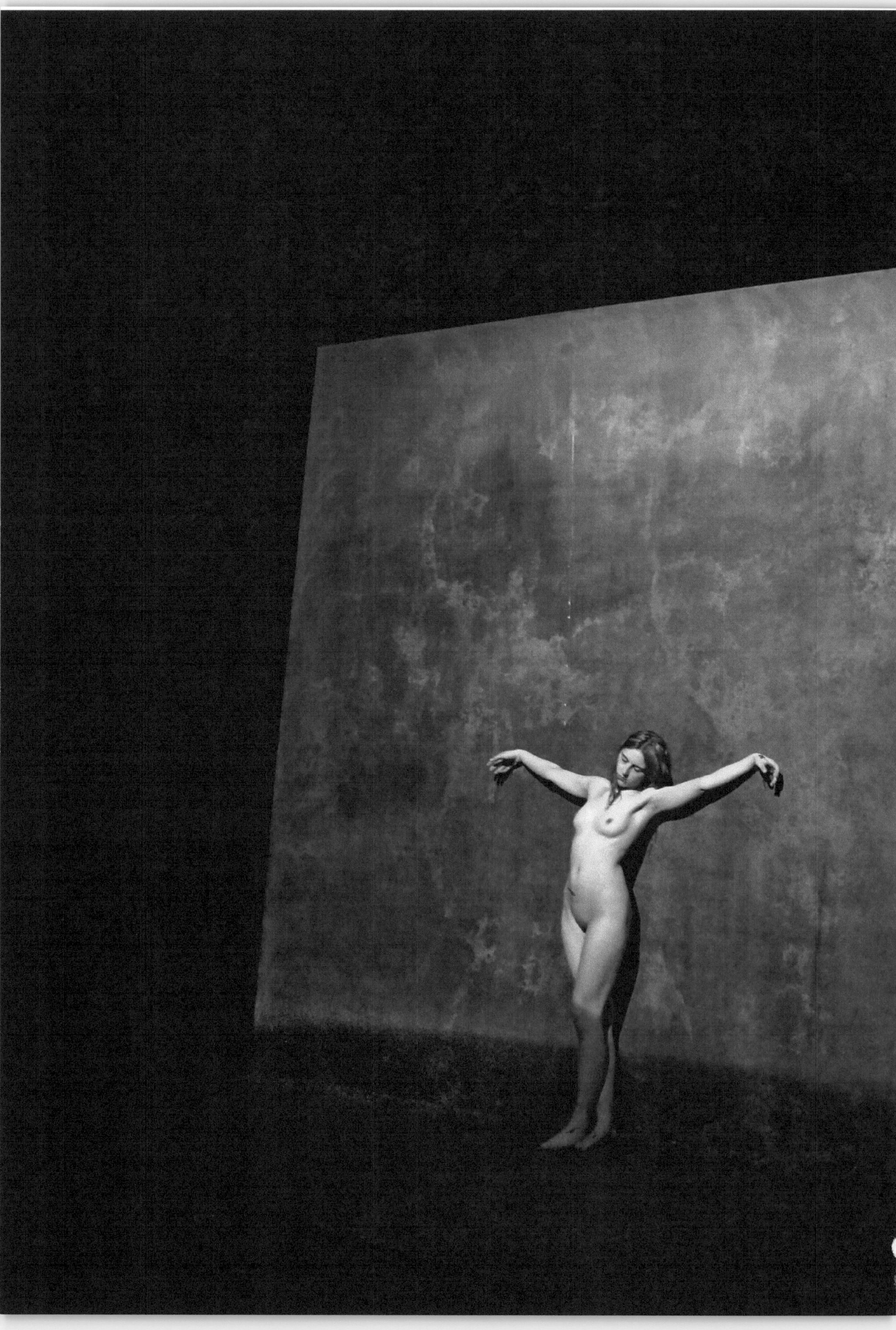

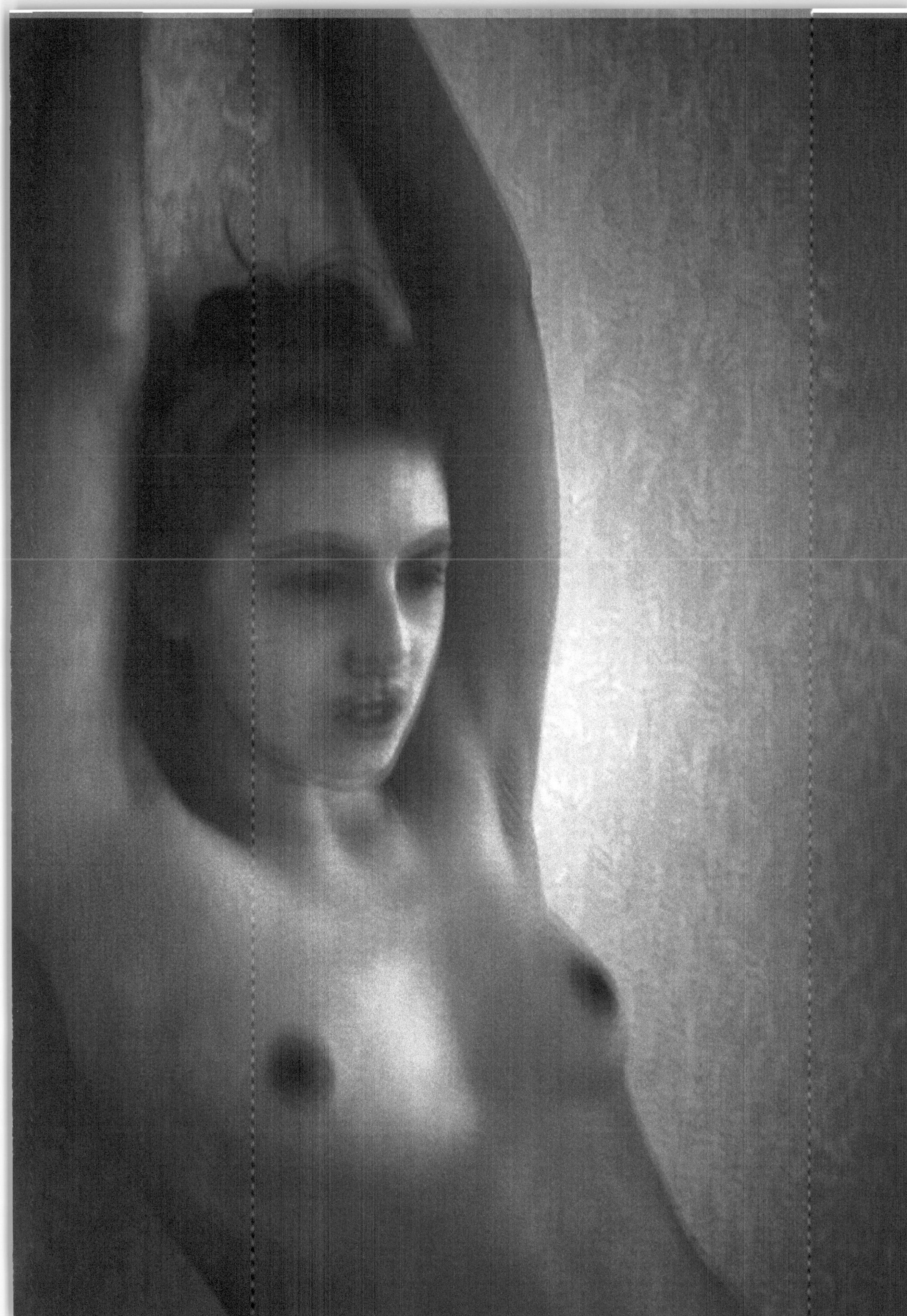

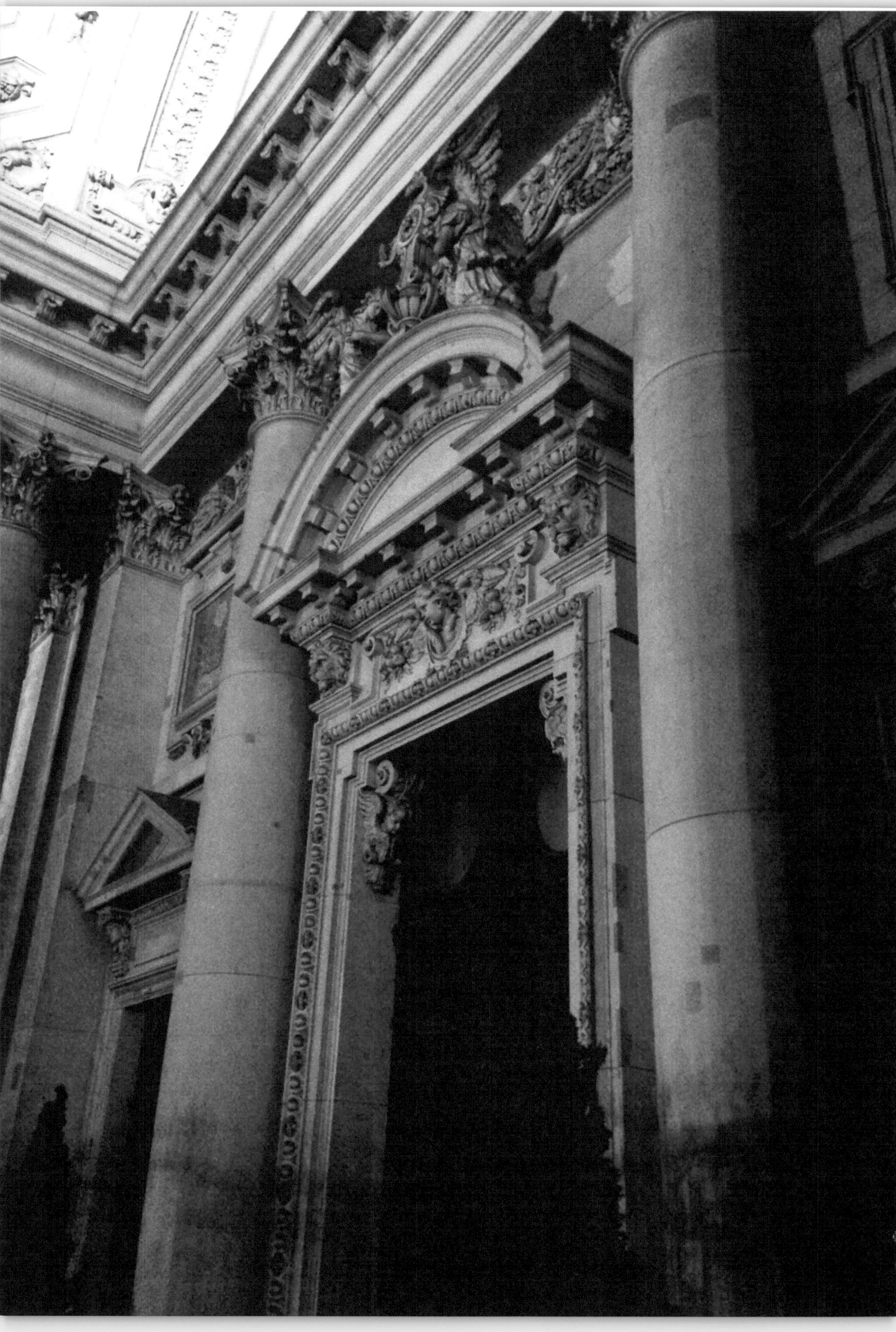

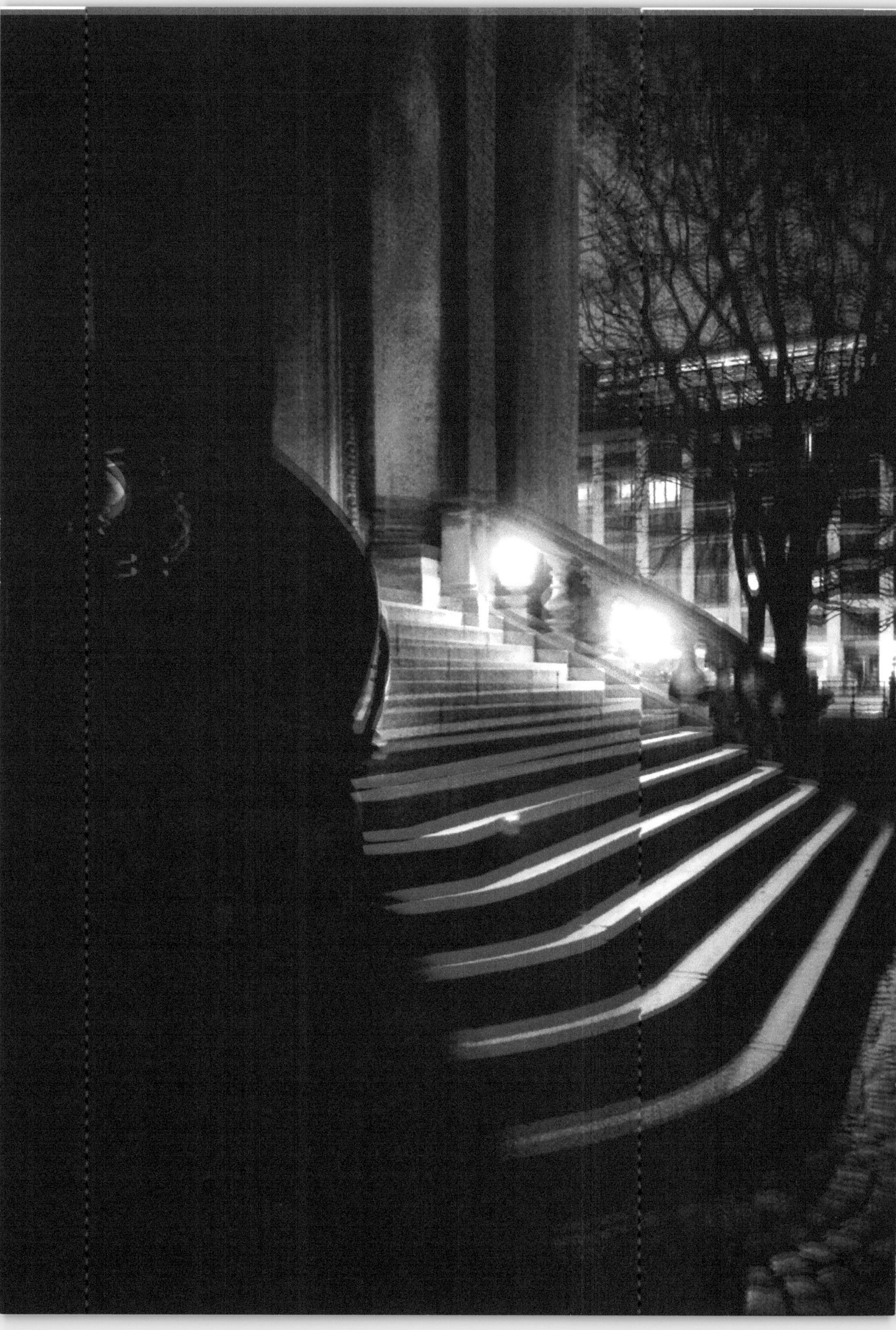

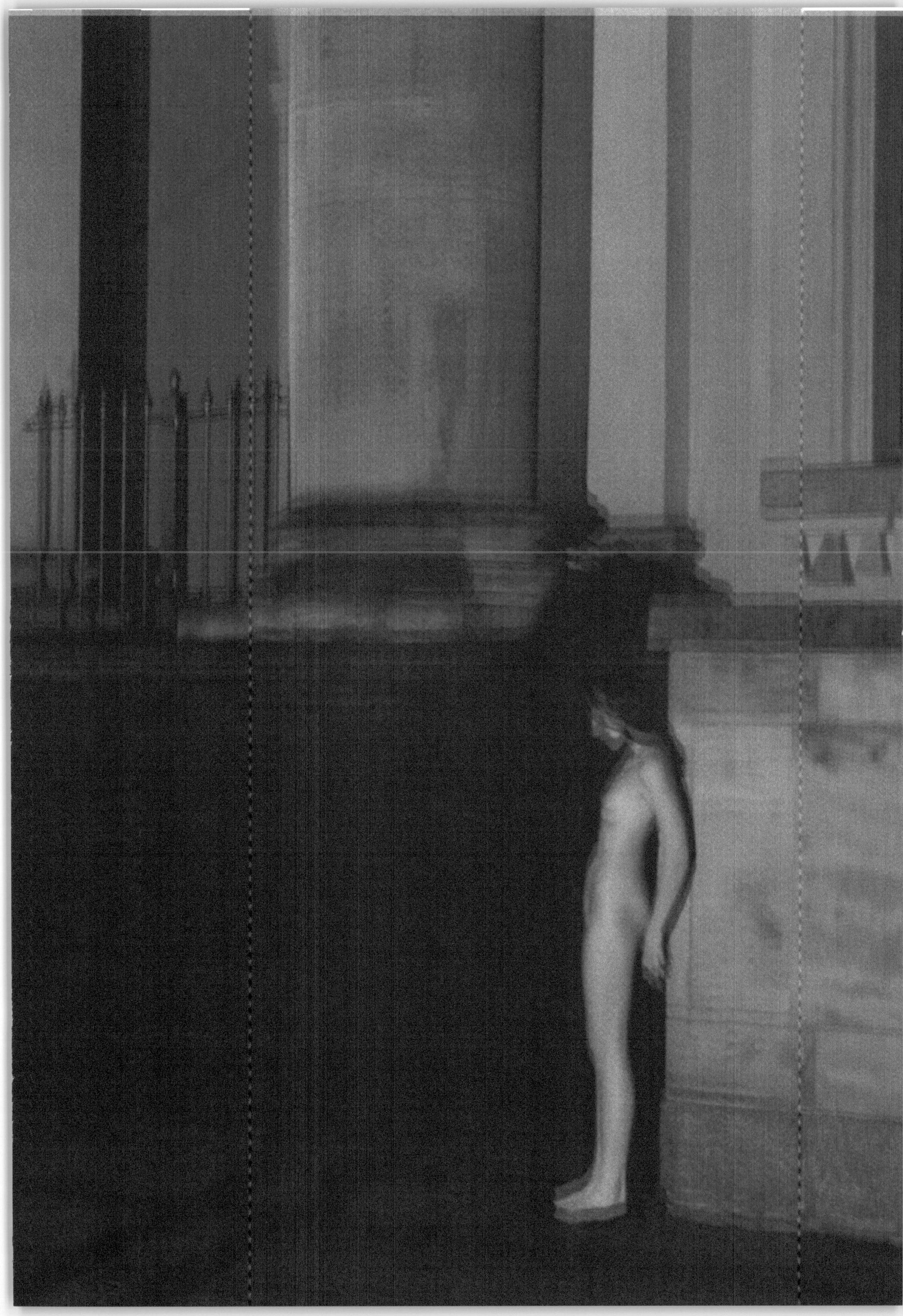

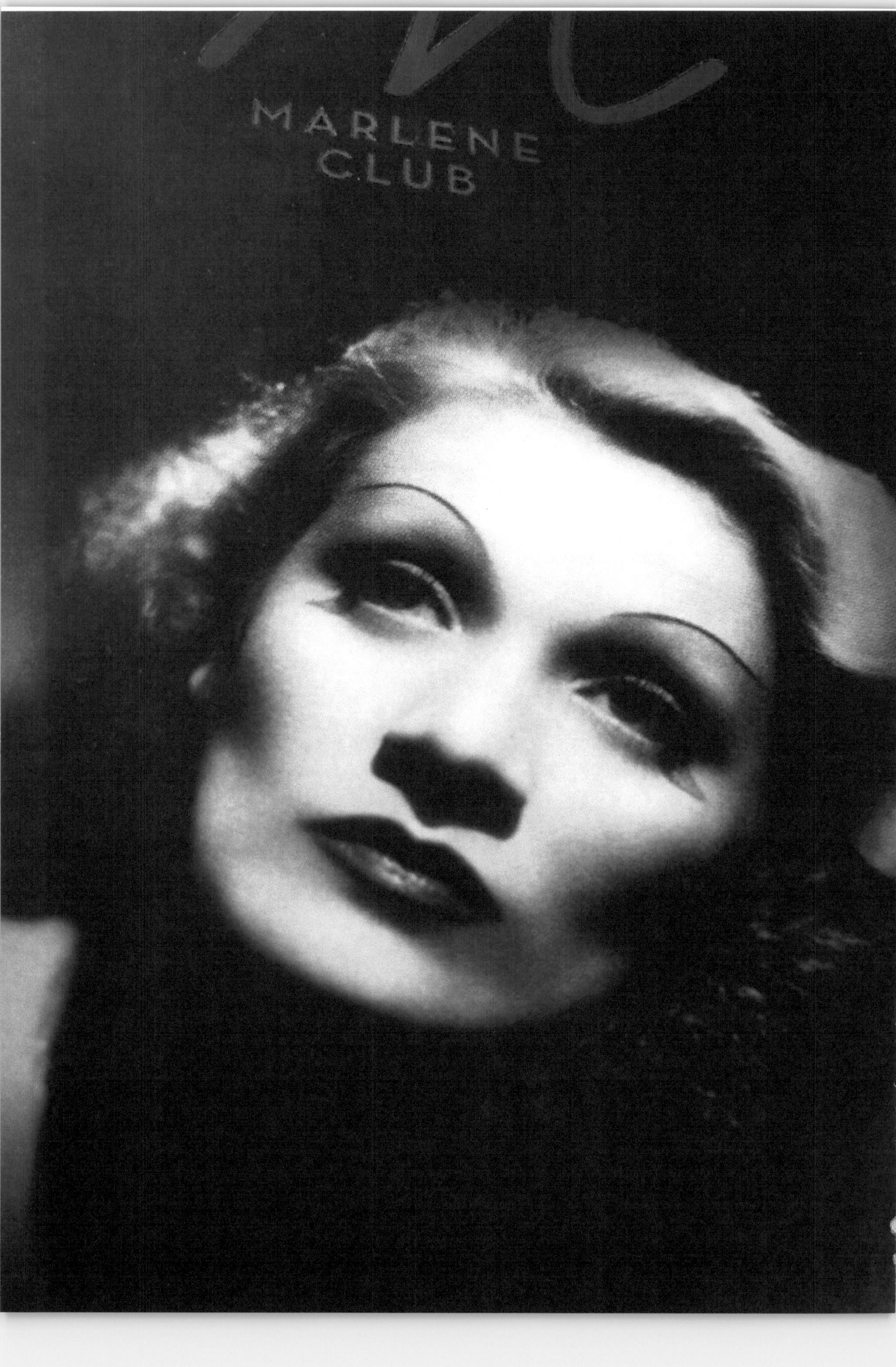
MARLENE
CLUB

www.ingramcontent.com/pod-product-compliance
Lightning Source LLC
Chambersburg PA
CBHW051932210526
45473CB00006B/2222